A GARDEN'S PROMISE

Spiritual Reflections
on Growing from the Heart

JUDITH COUCHMAN

ILLUSTRATIONS BY JOEL SPECTOR

WATERBROOK
PRESS

COLORADO SPRINGS

A GARDEN'S PROMISE

Published by WaterBrook Press
5446 North Academy Boulevard, Suite 200
Colorado Springs, Colorado 80918
A division of Bantam Doubleday Dell Publishing Group, Inc.

Published in association with the literary agency of
Alive Communications, Inc., 1465 Kelly Johnson Blvd.
Suite 320, Colorado Springs, Colorado 80920

Scriptures in this book, unless otherwise noted,
are from the *New International Version*
© 1973, 1984 by International Bible Society,
used by permission of Zondervan Publishing House

· Other versions used:
New American Standard Bible (NASB)
© 1960, 1977 by the Lockman Foundation
The Holy Bible, New Century Version (NCV)
© 1987, 1988, 1991 by Word Publishing, Dallas, Texas 75234
The New Revised Standard Version Bible (NRSV)
© 1989 by the Division of Christian Education
of the National Council of the Churches of Christ
in the United States of America
King James Version (KJV)

ISBN 1-57856-010-1
©1997 by Judy C. Couchman
Pastel illustrations ©1997 by Joel Spector
Cover and interior design by D² DesignWorks

January 1998—First Edition
1   3   5   7   9   10   8   6   4   2

For Millie and Jeannie,

*my father's sisters who've grown us
a legacy in the garden*

Also by Judith Couchman

The Woman Behind the Mirror

Shaping a Woman's Soul

Designing a Woman's Life Bible Study

Designing a Woman's Life

Lord, Please Help Me to Change

Lord, Have You Forgotten Me?

Why Is Her Life Better Than Mine?

If I'm So Good, Why Don't I Act That Way?

Getting a Grip on Guilt

Compilations by Judith Couchman

Only Trust Him (Dwight L. Moody)

For Me to Live Is Christ (Charles Spurgeon)

Growing Deeper with God (Oswald Chambers)

Anywhere He Leads Me (Corrie ten Boom)

Dare to Believe (Smith Wigglesworth)

Loving God with All Your Heart (Andrew Murray)

A Very Present Help (Amy Carmichael)

CONTENTS

The Everyday Gardener

The Faithful Garden

Aside from the author, every book needs a visionary—a person determined to bring its message to readers in the most effective way possible. Without a doubt, Rebecca Price, vice president of WaterBrook Press, has been the visionary for *A Garden's Promise*. Thanks, Rebecca, for believing in my idea, spreading enthusiasm within your company, and painstakingly ensuring that the cover and interior designs look beautiful. Your quest for quality is a treasured gift.

Thanks also to Traci Mullins for expertly editing the text and warmly expressing her confidence in my work, to Carol Bartley for her copyediting acumen, and to David Uttley for his art direction and Joel Spector for the beautiful garden illustrations.

I am in humble debt to my prayer team members who not only interceded for this project, but took a special interest because most of them are gardeners: Charette Barta, Win Couchman, Madalene Harris, Karen Hilt, Nancy Lemons. Other praying gardeners were my mother and sister, Opal Couchman and Shirley Honeywell.

There were also gardeners who reviewed the manuscript, gave input, and kept me on track with its how-to advice. I offer a big thanks to Win Couchman, Karen Hilt, Shirley Honeywell, Pat Schultz, and Georgia Shaffer. May this book give to all of these nature lovers the nurture they've so generously handed to me.

Though there are too many names to mention here, I'm grateful to additional friends, relatives, and acquaintances who've inspired me toward the necessity of creating beauty and replenishing my soul in the garden. By example, they've encouraged me to cast aside work and lose my worries to nature. Most important, they've taught me that God walks in the garden, calls my name, and waits for me to join Him.

The Promise of Pleasure

As a new flower gardener several years ago, I scoured for answers to my horticultural questions, all of which were embarrassingly basic. What was the difference among annuals, biennials, and perennials? What, exactly, was compost, and why did I need such smelly stuff? When and how could I plant bulbs? How often should I water? And what in the world was a pH level?

From my ancestors I'd inherited an innate sense about planting the earth, but I still felt shy about asking nursery owners too many questions, though I frequently haunted their greenhouses and overspent my budget on flowers I knew little or nothing about. During planting season gardening shops brimmed with browsers and long lines of buyers, so there wasn't time for clerks to answer my questions. Or when I ventured a query or two, I rarely understood their replies. Most of the time, though, I didn't even know what questions to ask.

Being a reader by nature and a writer by profession, I turned to gardening books for information and solace. In their pages I uncovered the crucial questions, answered them, and applied the principles to my small yard. Sometimes I followed the authors' advice to the detail, but more frequently I used their guidelines to backdrop my own version of winging it. Even with a stack of gardening books, I was still flying somewhat blind, partly because I'm intuitive and avoid enforced structure, partly because the experts' instructions were too expensive, complicated, or time-consuming for a beginning gardener like me, who could only spend here-and-there time in the yard.

The garden's allure and mystery dispelled my need to know everything and do everything "just right."

So what kept me going? I loved the earthiness of cultivating soil; the hunt for flowers and tools and pots; the art of combining colors and textures and shapes and sizes; the surety of surprises and new beginnings; the gladness of burgeoning blooms; and most of all, the inexplicable connection to God and His earth. The garden's allure and mystery dispelled my need to know everything and do everything "just right." And though I still check those reference books, I've never allowed precision to overpower the pleasure of gardening. Because of this, I've created my share of floral flops, but that hasn't mattered. Gardening, for me, is the promise of joy.

As the gardening references piled up in my home office, though, I fantasized about the kind of guidance that would have helped and inspired me. I envisioned a book for gardening novices that imparted the basics in simple language, but also invited them to plunge into their backyards and abandonly create. No big productions; no urgency to perform; just a friendly voice that encouraged would-be gardeners to cast aside the fear of failure, the need for perfection, and the tendency to compare their modest flower beds to the magnificent photos in books written by horticulturists (though I respect professional gardeners' knowledge and admire their consummate gardens). A book that communicated inspiration rather than hard-to-achieve dictums.

So why don't you write it? The question emerged from within, and at first I protested. *I'm an author, not a professional gardener. There's an awful lot I don't know.*

That's exactly the point, came the reply. *For you gardening is about pleasure, not knowledge or perfection. Why not write about that?*

And so I did.

It's been said that "one is nearer God's heart in a garden than anywhere else on earth."[1] As someone who seeks to know her Creator, I heartily agree. Above the intrinsic joy of collaborating with the earth, I treasure the garden's spiritual lessons. Each gardening year I participate in the cycle of birth, death, and resurrection, comparing them to my inner journey and growth. (Who could miss the obvious spiritual parallels?) Tending flower beds has taught me about God and His character, the mysteries of a soul, my sin and the Father's forgiveness, the spirituality of perseverance, the certainty of eternity, and much more.

Naturally, then, as I wrote, I couldn't separate the thrill of the garden from the pleasure of God's presence. So aside from offering basic planting and maintaining instructions, this book centers on stories about gardening and how its principles showcase the profundity of life and spirituality. I believe that if we'll listen, gardening promises us not only God's love, but the Maker Himself. And He is the greatest pleasure of all.

> *Earth's crammed with heaven,*
> *And every common bush afire with God.*
> *And only he who sees take off his shoes.*[2]
>
> ELIZABETH BARRETT BROWNING, 1806-1861

In the Beginning

CELEBRATING THE ROOTS OF GARDENING

The land produced vegetation.... And God saw that it was good.

—GENESIS 1:12

CHAPTER ONE

Memories of Eden

The LORD God put the man in the garden
of Eden to care for it and work it.

—GENESIS 2:15, NCV

ore than anything, I must have flowers. Always, always," said the French painter Claude Monet.[1] Nearly a century later his Giverny gardens still flourish and testify to an artist's unquenchable love for cultivating the earth.

What is it about gardeners? What makes them so passionate, so enthralled? Whether it's flowers or vegetables, herbs or shrubbery, vast landscapes or blemished pots, what prompts us to till, impregnate, and harvest the earth? What compels us to sweat and grow weary again and again? Why do we babble about tools and bulb catalogs? Or rise early to stroll through the mist, clutching steaming coffee mugs, searching for new growth?

What is it? I ask while pulling the umpteenth weed, but I already know the answer. *It's in our blood,* I remember as I straighten up, stretch my back, and survey the yard.

In my case gardening hovers as an inherited family interest as natural as waking in the morning. Though I never met her, I cherish stories about my maternal grandmother toiling in her gardens despite poverty and the chaos of six children. Vegetables as provisions; flowers for beauty. Yes, for Grandma beauty was necessary. She eked out money for seeds and swapped cuttings with neighbors to splash color across her Depression-era yard. Even today peonies frame her grave, but like Monet, flowering bushes aren't her greatest legacy.

No, not flowers, but people. Her children and grandchildren. We constitute her most valuable endowment. Grandma lives through the generations who resemble her physically and emotionally, those who inherited her tastes and talents, attitudes and propensities. We carry her genetic personality, and for many of us, her love for gardening. The dancer Martha Graham called this "blood memory." We harbor within us the characteristics of our ancestors.

Mystics understand that gardening is a spiritual experience. It draws us closer to God.

I understand what the famous dancer meant. My childhood memories fill with my mother's loving obsession with tending flower beds, a habit she still faithfully nurtures today. For years my sister Shirley planted vegetables to feed a growing family; now her yard sprawls with perennials, a symbol of an empty nest. My sister Barb grows flowers in a small plot, but what she really loves is mowing the grass. In our own and ordinary way, we each enjoy and reverence the earth.

Yet my family can't claim this compulsion to dig in the dirt as exclusive to our bloodlines. Since the beginning of time, flooding the centuries and coursing through our veins, humanity has heard the earth's call. Literally, its dust thrives in our blood. God formed us from the ground, and when we die, our bodies return to the soil. The years between, the span of our lifetimes, we're dependent on the earth for sustenance. We eat and drink from the ground's harvest, filling ourselves with its strength.

For the mystical among us, sifting the earth stirs veiled remembrances of our origins. Tending the ground evokes images of Eden, when humanity lived in a magnificent garden and walked intimately with the Creator. Mystics understand that gardening is a spiritual experience. It draws us closer to God.

With much pleasure, I resonate with all of these philosophical reasons for gardening: participating in my family's inheritance, remembering my place in the earth, growing closer to God. Yet when people ask, "Why do you spend so much time gardening?" I simply reply, "I like gardening. It gives me joy." That answer satisfies them.

In my heart, though, I treasure the deeper reasons for gardening. They fill me with purpose and significance. They also justify my planting-season fever. As I drive to a local nursery for the third time in a day, I understand why "more than anything, I need flowers. Always, always."

Gardening also recalls that God created us in His image. In Genesis He said, "Let us make human beings in our image and likeness" (1:26, NCV). We create gardens because we're fashioned after the Artist who designed cornstalks and viney tomatoes, multihued tulips and sprightly columbines, chocolate mint and creeping rosemary.

We create because God created, and with Him we share the responsibility of tending the earth. After shaping the first man in His likeness, God told him, "Fill the earth and be its master" (verse 28, NCV). Then God looked at everything He created and called it good. He felt pleased.

As we ponder our earth-grown creations, we can remember that God raised up human life and sustained it in a garden. And when we tend our plots, no matter their size or abundance, we can feel His pleasure.

A Prayer of Gratitude

Oh God, my bountiful Creator, thank You for the gift of the garden. As I turn the soil, remind me of Your love; as I gather up flowers, draw me closer to You. Thank You for the work of tending the earth. As I view the garden's yield, mingle my joy with Yours. Amen.

Into the Garden
TO GROW OR NOT TO GROW?

Gardens vary as much as the people who tend them. So what kind of gardening will suit you? Any of these possibilities can prove rewarding.

 ANNUALS. These flowers bloom all summer, but unless they self-sow their seeds, annuals don't reappear the next growing season. Still, they gather into quick, colorful gardens with moderate upkeep.

 BULBS. Growing bulbs requires faith. There are many types of bulbs, planted at varying times of the year, but traditionally they're buried in the fall, lie dormant over the winter, and push up from the springtime ground. The colors look glorious, and once bulbs take root, they visit the awakening garden year after year.

 HERBS. A good choice for avid cooks, herbs serve as recipe ingredients, healing agents, and ornaments in the kitchen. Some are annuals, some perennials, depending on the climate. Herbs can be low-maintenance plants and, when dried out, enjoyed all year.

 PERENNIALS. Consider these flowers the "old faithfuls" of the garden. They appear each growing season, often larger and more beautiful than the previous year. However, perennials need the passage of a dormant winter season before they "show off" in size and then bloom for only days or weeks. The rest of the season their foliage provides green accents in the garden.

 POTS. Plant them with annuals and greenery. Place them on the deck, in a window box, around patios, both in shady and sunny locations, depending on the plants' need for light. Flowers in pots, especially terra cotta ones, ask for frequent watering.

 SHRUBBERY. Think of bonsai plants and sculptured bushes. Or the hedge that lends privacy to the yard. Growing shrubs can be satisfying, but as with perennials, be prepared to invest a few years before they increase in size.

 VEGETABLES. It's rewarding to eat from the labor of our hands. It's also time-consuming to tend a vegetable garden: planting, watering, feeding, inspecting for pests, keeping out hungry animals, harvesting crops before they spoil. But still, the results taste delicious!

CHAPTER TWO

Gardening for the Soul

He restores my soul.
—PSALM 23:3

One of my horticultural bibles is *The Garden Primer* by Barbara Damrosch, who describes the mysterious lure of gardening as well as anybody. "Gardening, for all of its down-to-earthness, has always had some mystery about it," she explains.

"Try as we may, I don't think we will ever shed so much light on gardening that we dampen the awe a gardener feels when the first vegetable seedlings start to come up in the spring," says Damrosch. "We may never explain things like why we are attracted to flowers just as butterflies and bees are, even though normally we have no role in their pollination. Perhaps their form and fragrance are somehow luring us to some fateful role in their survival. I don't think we'll ever know all there is about gardening, and I'm just as glad there will always be some magic about it."[2]

A "magic" about gardening is its ability to restore the soul. After even a short time in the garden, aside from the satisfaction of physical exercise, my head feels cleared, my inner person revived. The worries and frustrations I carry into the yard vanish while pulling weeds, rearranging plantings, or accomplishing other pulling, pushing, plopping, and pruning activities. It seems the opposite should be true—that with a mind free to wander, I'd fuss and fume about this and that, turning problems into uncatchable apparitions determined to annoy me. Instead, I leave the garden at peace.

One summer while a developmental project at my job delivered crisis after crisis, I especially turned to the garden for therapy. Each time a potentially insurmountable problem arose I tilled up more soil and planted something. "See that herb bed?" I asked visitors to my home. "That's when we were waiting for an answer about funding." Or, "Do you like the shade garden under my office window? That's when we thought the project might die." Or, "How about those potted geraniums along the outer sidewalk? That's when a certain staff person was making my life difficult."

Whenever the garden provides a way to replenish us, we have been gardening for the soul.

Not long ago I met a woman who, as one of the first in the nation to receive a bone marrow transplant for breast cancer, gathered comfort and emotional healing in the garden. When the recovery process seemed to drag on endlessly, Georgia created Mourning Glory Gardens at her home in Pennsylvania and discovered with the psalmist, "Those who sow in tears will reap with songs of joy" (Psalm 126:5). They can celebrate in the garden.

Today Georgia Shaffer speaks publicly about "gardening for the soul" and suggests that when we cultivate nature, we open ourselves to its ability to heal the inner person. Georgia says, "Whether your garden is in the sun, shade, or a container, gardening can help keep you mentally, physically, emotionally, and spiritually healthy. You can garden for the soul as you cultivate your special place of beauty and the most important personal relationship of all—your relationship with God."[3]

Georgia's thoughts resonate in the lives of every gardener I know. They understand that gardening touches something deep within. A friend of mine who survived an emotionally bloody school year, both as a teacher and a mother, confided to me, "I think I'll be okay for a while now. It's summer and I have mornings in the garden."

Of course, we don't have to be physically and emotionally depleted to partake of the garden's soulish reassurances. Nor do we have to be *working* in the garden. The garden is also a place to play, sing, relax, chat, eat, read, meditate, entertain, or as a friend of mine who likes to sit and think about nothing, says, "veg out." Whenever the garden provides a way to replenish us, we have been gardening for the soul.

In the beginning of time, God walked through a garden in the evening's coolness, calling for Adam and Eve, desiring fellowship with His loved ones (Genesis 3:8). I believe He still walks in gardens today, whispering our names, waiting for us to join Him. I accept as truth the words to a hymn of my youth:

> *I come to the garden alone, while the dew is still on the roses;*
> *And the voice I hear, falling on my ear, the Son of God discloses.*
> *And He walks with me, and He talks with me, and He tells me I am His own,*
> *And the joy we share as we tarry there, none other has ever known.*[4]

Truly, this is gardening for the soul.

Into the Garden
A Place of Surprise and Solace

By Martha Stewart

A true garden grows forever: there are always new trees to place, new seeds to sow.

But for me, the garden is not just a place to grow things . . . a garden is also a place where one can walk and think, sit and contemplate. A garden should have surprises, and offer solace.

My own garden has its secrets: I love to share them with friends who come to enjoy the beauty and quiet of the place. The swamp maple tree that grows by the road in front of the house has a peculiar branch that has somehow grown into another, creating a kind of natural tie.

The "Lavender Lassie" rose has reverted in part to its "Blaze" root stock, resulting in a climber that is half red, half purple. The steps up to the raised rose bed behind the barn are really rocks jutting out from the stone wall, copied from an old staircase I saw in Tuscany.

The "Veilchhenblau" rose bush is climbing up the giant shagbark hickory and will soon cover over a glaring scar.

Most of all, the garden is a place where I learn. Gardening is a humbling experience. Mistakes are often made, but they can be corrected with few or no lasting effects. I was always a very impatient person. I thought that by force of will I could get things done immediately; gardening has taught me patience. Nature, with her timetables, cannot be rushed.

And yet, I never begrudge the effort, because gardening teaches a sense of optimism and hope for the future.

I think I may be a better person for having given serious time and thought and effort to gardening. I am proud of having learned to work with nature to encourage beauty in my backyard. The hours I have spent cultivating the soil, weeding and planting, and just looking at what has come to be have given me boundless pleasure.

I no longer say, "I have to work in the garden today."

I say with deep contentment, "I'm gardening today." I have truly reaped the bounty of the garden.[5]

CHAPTER THREE

The Pleasure of the Process

*There is nothing better for a man
than to enjoy his work.*

—ECCLESIASTES 3:22

I n the late 1950s the revered editor Katharine S. White began writing a series of fourteen articles on gardening for *The New Yorker,* sprung from her love for perusing seed catalogs and planting the "finds" from her research. Her surprised husband, the writer E. B. White, had never considered Katharine an expert on horticultural matters but conceded that her self-taught gardening knowledge rivaled that of gardening professionals.

However, writing about gardening was another matter. In his introduction to Katharine's book, *Onward and Upward in the Garden,* a posthumous compilation of the popular articles, E. B. wrote, "Katharine's act of composition often achieved the turbulence of a shoot-out. The editor in her fought the writer every inch of the way; the struggle was felt all through the house. She would write eight or ten words, then draw her gun and shoot them down."

To her husband's delight, Katharine's near-death encounters with horticultural writing paid off. Her articles met with enthusiasm, and she developed a loyal readership through the years. But for Katharine, it was the act of gardening—not merely writing about gardening—that produced immeasurable satisfaction.

Katharine enjoyed the process of gardening as much or more than its outcome, and she spontaneously visited her flower beds whenever the mood hit her. E. B. described his wife as a "spur-of-the-moment escapee from the house." He reminisced, "I seldom saw [Katharine] *prepare* for gardening, she merely wandered out into the cold and the wet, into the sun and the warmth, wearing whatever she had put on that morning. Once she was drawn into the fray, once involved in transplanting or weeding or thinning or pulling deadheads, she forgot all else; her clothes had to take things as they came. I, who was the animal husbandryman on the place, in blue jeans and an old shirt, used to marvel at how unhesitatingly she would kneel in the dirt and begin grubbing about, garbed in a spotless cotton dress or handsome tweed skirt and jacket. She simply refused to dress *down* to a garden; she moved in elegantly and walked among her flowers as she walked among her friends—nicely dressed, perfectly poised. If when she arrived back indoors the Ferragamos were encased in muck, she kicked them off. If the tweed suit was a mess, she sent it to the cleaner's."[6]

Whether we dress the part in boots or arrive unexpectedly in designer shoes, most of all gardening is about enjoying the work, not just the results, which a seasoned gardener will admit is never finished. (There is always one more weed to pull, another space to fill.)

If we free ourselves to enjoy the work,…then most likely the garden will satisfy us for a lifetime.

If we don't find pleasure in the process of gardening—of plotting and planting, of experimenting and exhausting our resources but nonetheless feeling grand—then we've missed the point. We've disembarked at the Shoot-Out Corral, and before we kill our spirits, we should probably adopt a different pastime.

On the other hand, gardening can teach us to savor the moments. If we free ourselves to enjoy the work, to love what we do while we're doing it, then most likely the garden will satisfy us for a lifetime. Writing aside, Katharine knew how to participate wholly in the moment. Ferragamos and all, she's an example we can follow.

Although we wrestle with the truth of it, spiritual growth constitutes a lifetime process—a day-by-day, hour-by-hour decision to live, learn, and change as we walk with God. Though at times we experience the miraculous, we usually grow through the determination of a slow plod. Yet the work of spiritual growth needn't be always agonizing. We can cherish our moments in prayer and the Scriptures, for we sit with the loving, giving Father.

God the Father wants to fulfill our desires, if we place Him first in our hearts, especially when we long to be holy. The psalmist advised, "Delight yourself in the LORD and he will give you the desires of your heart. Commit your way to the LORD; trust in him and he will do this" (Psalm 37:4-5). Trusting God, we too can live in the moments.

A Prayer for the Moments

Oh, God, teach me to cherish the moments of my life. Open my eyes to the wonder of each day, each hour, and how Your goodness surrounds me. Just as I enjoy the process of gardening, I want to delight in the dailiness of spiritual growth and the surety of Your presence. Amen.

THE WELL-DRESSED GARDENER

Though we need to create our own gardening clothing style—whatever feels functional and comfortable for us—these suggestions for garden dressing may help the process.

▪ BOOTS & SHOES. The key feature for footwear is its ability to repel dirt, water, and mud. These range from army to hiking to Wellie boots which reach up to the knees. Or if boots feel klunky, try rubber shoes called "mud flats" or clogs or other gardening shoes in shops or catalogs.

▪ GARDENING GLOVES. Rubber or pigskin gloves repel the water and dirt but minimize the ability to feel the earth. They also get hot. Cotton gloves provide more feeling and air circulation but soak in the dirt and wetness and need the long cycle in the washer. For certain projects, some gardeners prefer elbow-high or thorn-resistant gloves. Others eschew gloves altogether, preferring to touch the dirt.

▪ HATS & SCARVES. Whatever keeps the sun and wind out of the eyes and hair, and solar heat from burning the scalp, suits a gardener. Try a straw hat, a baseball cap, an old scarf. Sweatbands help when the temperature heats up.

▪ RAIN GEAR. If a temporary drizzle falls, a rain poncho or slicker covers the head and body, while leaving the arms and hands room to stretch. Or try an old raincoat and cap.

▪ SHIRTS & PANTS. Gardeners who work all day may prefer dressing in layers, discarding the top clothes as the day warms up. Cotton pants and shirts with sleeves protect the body well, as do denims and overalls. Wearing shorts means a case of grass- and dirt-stained "gardening knees" and insect bites. Skinny T-shirts and halter tops beg trouble from the sun and dirt.

▪ OPTIONAL ITEMS. Knee pads prevent wearing out pants too soon. A multipocket vest or apron can carry small tools. Other personal essentials might be hand wax for moisture and protection, insect repellent for warding off bugs, sunglasses for the brightest times of day, sunscreen for guarding against burns and skin cancer, a water bottle for slaking thirst, and a clock set away from the dirt and moisture.

CHAPTER FOUR

Even the Best-Laid Plans

My times are in your hands.

—PSALM 31:15

I had probably read *House and Garden* and *Metropolitan Home* too much, so maybe my expectations had grown unrealistic, but several summers ago I created ambitious plans for remodeling the yard and pushed myself toward them.

When I'd moved into this house a year earlier, the yard was a cross between a jungle and a desert. While weeds and spindly perennials strangled the outer edges, parched and barren brown spots decorated the lawn. I knew it would take time and work to restore the property to its original beauty, and a wise friend suggested that I hire someone to help. Except for a rototilling and tree-pulling Saturday in March, I ignored the recommendation.

In her book *Green Thoughts,* the writer and gardener Eleanor Perényi had told me, "Well-trained gardeners who like their work must live [somewhere] in America, but not around here and not in my price range. When I look back at the long process of eccentrics, young and old, foreign and domestic, who have worked for me, I wonder how I and the garden have survived their ministrations."[7] She then described numerous hired workers who had regressed or ruined her gardens.

"None of that for me," I pronounced with an air of certainty that only the ignorant possess. I decided to tackle the work myself, despite a weak back and a book deadline. I pulled up weeds, hacked at vines, transplanted grass, dug out flower beds, hauled around compost, erected a small greenhouse, inset stone edgings, shopped at nurseries, planted a few hundred flowers, initiated an herb garden, poured out red bark, spread sheep manure, conducted minor mulch marathons, and set out colorfully planted terra cotta pots and window boxes.

The potential beauty motivated me, but so did two approaching events, and perhaps my pride. I'd accepted an invitation to speak at a conference in mid-June and wanted to complete the yard work by that time. This would offer the flowers plenty of time to grow lush for a business commitment: a backyard barbecue in July. It was a perfect plan.

I finished the yard; I attended the conference; and while I was gone, a hailstorm shredded my gardens. With nary a blossom in sight—but plenty of debris in the yard—the setback felt like starting all over again. So with a compassionate friend and an attack of the blues, I spent a day cleaning up messes. A few weeks later the barbecue that had compelled me to finish planting was canceled. All that work, all that stress, for a devastated yard with nothing to preen about.

Looking out my office window that September, though, it was hard to imagine why I'd felt so upset. In the gardens, flowers bent with blossoms and herbs escaped the boundaries of their beds. With food, water, and pruning, nature recovered from itself. In addition to the hail, the yard also survived several bouts with bugs, too much rain, and repeated chilly nights. In spite of the weather, in spite of me, it grew with abandon.

In the garden not all of our plans materialize, nor does everything grow in a straight line.

The garden's resiliency amazes me.

Thinking about the yard's comeback that summer, I remind myself that in the garden not all of our plans materialize, nor does everything grow in a straight line. But we can train and nurture the unwieldy growth—and confront the bugs, drought, and storms that rail against it—until someday, with luscious curves and color, it rebounds and blooms again. Despite our best-laid plans.

Accordingly, we can view personal and spiritual setbacks as temporary challenges rather than permanent defeats. Gardening has taught me that when my plans don't work there is always another route to joy, if I'm willing to stay flexible and keep cultivating. With help from heaven, the human soul can rebound, and I need not give up hope.

It is true, though, that ultimately we can't control everything about our lives. We can't avoid the inevitability of detours and disappointments, even some destruction. But God has promised to cultivate us anew, healing and mending our brokenness, making our lives more bountiful than before.

He has promised, "I will make up to you for the years that the swarming locust has eaten. . . . And you shall have plenty to eat and be satisfied, and praise the name of the LORD your God, who has dealt wondrously with you; then My people will never be put to shame" (Joel 2:25-26, NASB).

After a summer of killing bugs, I can attest to the profundity of that promise.

A Prayer of Gratitude

Lord, just as I can't control the weather's ways or the garden's timetables, I acknowledge that I'm not the one who ultimately manages my life. My times are in Your hands. So this is my act of letting go and allowing You to direct my destiny. Amen.

———

For those of us who prefer planning, drawing a to-scale scheme on graph paper is the way to begin a garden. We can plot the types of flowers to buy, according to the sizes and shapes indicated in the plan. Planners often prefer carefully groomed gardens, with clean borders and breathing space between plants, the characteristics of a formal or Japanese garden.

If the idea of precise planning feels rigid, then the decide-as-you-go method may work better. We can form a rough idea in our heads, make amendable lists of what to buy, and decide what goes where as we move along. As a result, we may prefer an unrestrained, informal garden or a wildflower meadow.

However we proceed, we can ask these questions when choosing a site.

▪ DRAINAGE. When it rains, will the water run off, or do some spots need grading so excess water won't suffocate plant roots?

▪ HISTORY. What vegetation already thrives in this area?

▪ SOIL. What type of soil currently exists in the yard?

▪ SUNLIGHT. How much sun and shade does this site receive each day?

▪ TEMPERATURE. How hot is the planting site? What is the temperature's range?

▪ WATER. Aside from rainfall, how will the beds be watered?

After choosing a site we can employ these elements of good design.

▪ COLORS. Blooms can be hot (reds, yellows, oranges) or cool (blues, greens, lavenders), complementary or analogous, or multicolored.

▪ SHAPE. Flowering bushes, shrubs, and trees present varying shapes, adding focal points and a sense of openness or depth.

▪ SIZE. Check the nursery's labels for the height and breadth of plants, placing the taller flowers in back and shorter ones in front.

▪ SMELL. For a sensory garden, choose trees, bushes, and flowers that emit a variety of pleasing scents.

▪ TEXTURE. Foliage can be rough or smooth and combined to create variety.

The Determined Quest for Beauty

God . . . richly provides us with
everything for our enjoyment

— I TIMOTHY 6:17

W hen my Grandma Storey decided to grow flowers in her yard, she tackled the project in her usual nonstop, no-nonsense style. Frances worked vigorously at planning, digging, and planting the huge flower bed and enlisted several of her children for the schlepping.

"It was quite the garden," recalled Uncle Marvin, who as the oldest son probably shouldered much of the physical burden. "When she finished, though, it dawned on Mother that she'd created a significant problem." Without the advantage of plumbing, there was no efficient way to water the flowers except to carry buckets back and forth, back and forth, from the water pump to the garden. Besides, the bucket method splashed rather than sprinkled the water, dumping it on delicate flowers, damaging petals and breaking stems, especially when she assigned impatient children to the task.

According to my uncle, his mother was not a woman to be beaten or bowed. Frances recruited her soft-spoken but deliberate husband to solve the problem, and from a practical standpoint, he did. In the middle of the flower bed, George constructed a tank that distributed water gently and evenly over his wife's cultivated soil. Finished with his creation and proud of it, he demonstrated it for Frances.

"It's ugly," she said, missing the technical ingenuity. No self-respecting gardener would tolerate a tin monstrosity protruding from her flower bed. He had to change the design. Exasperated, my grandfather refused, and once he decided, that was that.

Not to be defeated, Grandmother brought viney flowers from the fields and trained them to grow up and around the tank, and by midsummer the eyesore had transformed into a lovely, though oddly shaped, sculpture.

While listening to my uncle's story, with chagrin I identified with my grandmother. Only months before I'd participated in a similar scenario with a friend. Joe painted houses for a living, and one day he discovered two abandoned flower window boxes at a job site. Thinking these old boxes would fulfill my desire for gardening from the kitchen window, he lugged them into my place, beaming with the pride of discovery.

I thanked Joe for his thoughtfulness and then pronounced, "Well, I can use *that* one but not *this* one." Joe tried to convince me that both boxes were perfectly functional. I replied that yes, both were functional, but one of them looked unappealing. As the negotiation intensified, I used words like "pitiful" and "downright ugly" to describe the rejected window box, and finally Joe acquiesced. He learned that just as one should never mess with Mother Nature, one should not interfere with a flower gardener's determined search for aesthetics.

If he were still alive, my Uncle Junior would agree. After fifty-plus years of marriage to Aunt Millie and a yard full of flowers, Junior knew if he wasn't going to

For the avid flower gardener, beauty is as essential as breathing.

join the beauty quest, he should clear out of the way. "Every time we visit a nursery we spend at least fifty dollars," he told me and sighed. Yet Junior took pride in Millie's gardening talent and their manicured yard, despite his need to fuss a bit about the expense. And yes, he devotedly helped his wife in the garden.

For the avid flower gardener, beauty is as essential as breathing, and it seems the more we plant, the more we desire the freshness of adding "just a few more" blooms to the beds. There is no sight like a lustrous and colorful garden, and nothing quite like the satisfaction of being its creator. But a beautiful garden can grow insatiable, and reluctantly I admit that we need an Uncle Junior around to remind of us our boundaries. We can't spend all of our time, all of our money, on the garden. We mustn't neglect the people in our lives or mow down their efforts to help us (though my Grandmother and I have tried).

In the garden, in all of life, we can learn when enough is enough and still bask in beauty.

Fortunately for us, God's pursuit of us knows and needs no boundaries, for His ways are always good. His love is limitless, and as the lover of our souls the Father spares no heavenly expense to draw us to Himself.

Through the prophet Jeremiah He proclaimed, "I have loved you with an everlasting love; I have drawn you with loving-kindness" (31:3). No matter who we are or what we have done, God's love can fashion us into spiritual beauties.

In Praise of Beauty

Lord, I praise You for Your beauty. I praise You for expressing Your beautiful character in an endless variety of blooms and colors and gardens throughout the world. I thank You for the beauty You've promised to create in me. Amen.

Into the Garden
A GARDENING-YEAR CALENDAR

Gardening's activities thread throughout the year. These flower gardening suggestions—based on a mild, four-season climate—spread across both nature's dormant and productive months. Adjust their timing according to your regional zone and local climate.

Spring
(March through May)

- Start seeds, thin seedlings indoors

- Move mulch from flower beds

- Transfer seedlings to harden off outdoors

- Remove dead flowers from bulbs

- Remove bulb foliage after it dies

- Inspect, repair watering system

- Pull up early weeds in the flower beds

- Add soil amendments to the flower beds

- Eradicate insects, diseases when they appear

- After last frost, plant seedlings, annuals, new perennials

- Divide established perennials, if needed

- Plant summer-blooming bulbs

Summer
(June through August)

- Pull weeds immediately

- Water flower beds as needed

- Fertilize flower beds, if desired

- Deadhead flowers to promote more blooms through the summer

- Add annuals to replace faded perennials

- Pinch back mums for full growth later

- Make entries in gardening journal

- Order fall bulbs and flowers

- Plant perennials for the fall

- Harvest herbs; make gifts or dry for later use

Fall
(September through November)

- Divide, transplant established perennials

- Plant new perennials

- Water plants deeply before they turn domant

- Dig up, take tender bulbs indoors

- Continue pulling weeds

- Cut back, clean up flower beds

- Add spent foliage to compost pile

- After first frost, plant spring-blooming bulbs

- Add amendments to flower beds

- Shut down watering system

- Bring in pots, window boxes, garden ornaments

- Create windbreaks for bushes and winter supports for vines

Winter
(December through February)

- When ground freezes, cover flower beds with mulch, if desired

- Check perennials for heaving (pulling up from roots when ground thaws)

- If ground thaws in mild climates, water bushes and perennials

- Begin a gardening journal for the new year

- Clean, repair gardening tools

- Purchase new gardening tools

- Stock up on gardening supplies

- Clean, refurbish pots, window boxes

- Request, review, order from seed, bulb catalogs

- Purchase, read gardening books for ideas, information

- Design flower beds for spring planting

- Create lists of flowers to plant next season

- Clean, order equipment/supplies for starting seeds indoors

IN THE ZONE

When you consider purchasing a plant, it helps to know whether it's expected to survive in your climate.

The U.S. Department of Agriculture divides North America into eleven zones, based on the regions' average minimum temperatures.

"To determine what plants will flourish in your garden, compare local weather-bureau temperatures with those in your garden, and consult garden-supply centers in your area; they sell what has proved to grow successfully."[8]

These are the average minimum winter temperatures for the zones.

- ZONE 1   Below -50° F
- ZONE 2   -50° F to -40° F
- ZONE 3   -40° F to -30° F
- ZONE 4   -30° F to -20° F
- ZONE 5   -20° F to -10° F
- ZONE 6   -10° F to 0° F
- ZONE 7   0° F to 10° F
- ZONE 8   10° F to 20° F
- ZONE 9   20° F to 30° F
- ZONE 10   30° F to 40° F
- ZONE 11   Above 40° F

Into the Garden
THE LITERARY GARDEN

———

Through the centuries writers have reflected on the garden's pleasure and meaning. Fortunately, many of their insights have survived the passage of time, and we can reflect on them too.

Do you resonate with any of these gardening sentiments?

This was one of my prayers: for a parcel of land not so very large, which should have a garden and a spring of everflowing water near the house, and a bit of woodland as well as these.[9]

—HORACE, 65-8 B.C.

God Almighty planted a garden; and, indeed, it is the purest of human pleasures.[10]

—FRANCIS BACON, 1561-1626

Ah yet, before I descend to the grave
May I a small house and large garden have;
And a few friends, and many books, both true,
Both wise, and both delightful too![11]

—ABRAHAM COWLEY, 1618-1667

My hoe as it bites the ground revenges my wrongs, and I have less lust to bite my enemies. In smoothing the rough hillocks, I soothe my temper.[12]

—RALPH WALDO EMERSON, 1803-1882

Flower in the crannied wall
I pluck you from out of the crannies
I hold you here, root and all, in my hand
Little flower—but if I could understand
What you are, root and all, and all in all
I should know what God and man is.[13]

—ALFRED, LORD TENNYSON, 1809-1892

A Garden is a lovesome thing.[14]

—THOMAS EDWARD BROWN, 1830-1897

He who is born with a silver spoon in his mouth is generally considered a fortunate person, but his good fortune is small compared to that of the happy mortal who enters this world with a passion for flowers in his soul.[15]

—CELIA THAXTER, 1835-1894

To own a bit of ground, to scratch it with a hoe, to plant seeds, and watch the renewal of life— this is the commonest delight of the race, the most satisfactory thing a man can do.[16]

—CHARLES DUDLEY WARNER, 1829-1900

Oh, Adam was a gardener,
and God who made him sees
That half a proper gardener's work
is done upon his knees.[17]

—RUDYARD KIPLING, 1865-1936

The Good Earth

CULTIVATING THE SOIL FOR BEAUTY

The earth is the LORD'S, and everything in it.

—PSALM 24:1

CHAPTER SIX

Soil, Toil, and Trouble

How is the soil? Is it fertile or poor?
—NUMBERS 13:20

I never imagined I'd want to read about dirt.

Not the stuff of tabloid magazines but the under-the-feet kind of earth that horticulturists call "soil." Then I became a gardener and life changed. Suddenly dirt mattered. I wanted my flowers to bloom in health, so I engaged in what I call "the toil of the soil." After digging up a flower bed, I dumped compost, manure, peat moss, and bone meal on the beds and worked it in with a hand cultivator.

Interestingly, I didn't arrive at this cause-and-effect activity by reading books or attending seminars. I didn't understand that the proper terminology for my actions was "improving the soil's structure" by "adding amendments." I didn't really know if my soil tactics were "right." But I was enthusiastic, and instinct told me I must do *something*, and after observing what other people bought at the gardening shops, I plunged into the earth.

Fortunately, my first flower beds bloomed well that summer, and it wasn't until later, after reading several gardening books, I discovered that my fervent digging of the beds and spreading of the manures had been misdirected. According to the experts, my flowers and

I were in trouble, along with my vocabulary usage and attitude toward the soil.

"Before trying to understand soil, stop thinking in such outmoded terms as 'the dirt under your feet,' or 'as common as dirt,'" a fat gardening tome began sternly. "Far from being common, soil is perhaps the most complex substance with which we must work to stay alive."[1] The authors then warned me not to add anything to the soil until after I tested it. My response was, *A test? What test?*

Several pages into the book I humbly confessed my sins against the soil but then noticed the authors dedicated nearly ninety pages to the topic. Other books were not as long, but their prose felt vague and complicated, often assuming too much knowledge for beginners like me. Horticulturists discussed humus, loam, and all things organic as if I'd heard of and loved them already, and I questioned my usually perceptive brain.

For example, I hesitated at explanations like this: "A substance such as dried blood, valuable as it is as the best organic fertilizer available, is worthless as a producer of the fibrous residue needed to build soil. Some substance such as lignin or cellulose is necessary to provide the long-lasting, porous remains that soil needs for aeration."[2]

What did this mean?

I don't want to disparage such books; I found helpful advice in them. But with little extra time on my hands, I crumbled at the prospect of so much to unearth about soil. Yet my desire to garden was strong, welling up in spite of the earth's complexities. So I opted for a slower approach to the ground. I decided that each gardening season I'd learn something new about soil, rather than tackling an all-at-once education. I'm certain some people will take issue with my solution (and I will

We don't have to know all the details and formulas to nurture successful gardens.

receive letters from them), but hopefully this confession will encourage fledgling flower growers to keep gardening instead of wilting along with their spent plants. Working the soil can be broken into simple steps, in understandable language, and we don't have to know all the details and formulas to nurture successful gardens.

Of course, learning the basics is still important; cultivated and nourished soil assists our flowers' prospects for flourishing. But if we don't take on the soil as an absolute passion (and few of us everyday gardeners do), we can view it as an anticipatory means to a much-desired end. Good soil equals beautiful blooms. And that makes sense to me.

Speaking to people from an agrarian culture, Jesus often used the ground as a metaphor for addressing the soul's condition. Was their spiritual soil hard and stony? Full of thorns and weeds? Then they needed to plow up and prepare the ground, making it healthy and receptive to God's truth. Otherwise, the seed of His Word would shrivel or choke, dying in the unforgiving dust.

The analogy still applies today. Good spiritual ground needs cultivation and constant attention, preventing the spirit from growing indifferent or dying, ensuring anticipation rather than dread about God's words to us. Whatever time, or cost, or learning process it requires, to flourish spiritually we need to break up our unplowed ground and not sow among thorns (Jeremiah 4:3).

For this, we are to be inexcusably passionate.

A Prayer of Preparation

Lord, when I prepare the ground for growth, grant me patience and understanding, anticipation and appreciation. As I break up the soil and enhance its fertility, I thank You for these preparatory times—for what they teach me about gardening, for what I learn about myself. Amen.

A RECIPE FOR GOOD GROUND

"The ideal soil for gardening— easy to work, and able to hold water and nutrients well—is loam. A crumbly balance of sand, silt, and clay, the particles of loam cling together in small roundish clumps, with abundant spaces between them to let air and water pass through."[3] Try these suggestions for preparing the soil for plant growth.

■ DETERMINE THE TEXTURE. Instead of loam, is the soil mostly clay, sand, or silt? A wash test, described later, can determine this. Gardeners can plant flowers that grow well in the existent soil type, or adapt the soil to other kinds of flowers they want to grow.

■ TEST FOR NUTRIENTS. Testing for nutrients identifies what type of fertilizer to use. Fertilizers can be added before planting a bed and at intervals throughout the season. See page 46 about pH soil testing and page 102 for fertilizers.

■ ADD SOIL AMENDMENTS. Amendments are additions to the soil that improve its "structure" or composition, enhancing its ability to produce healthy vegetation. They are added while digging a new plot or before planting seeds or flowers. Page 56 discusses soil amendments and page 60 explains composting.

A wash test, sometimes called a jar test, can determine how much sand, silt, and clay particles the soil contains.

■ FILL A QUART JAR with equal parts of soil and water. Shake the jar vigorously and let it stand for twenty-four hours. Sand will settle in a minute; silt in an hour; clay in a day.

■ MEASURE THE DEPTH of each layer. Divide by the total depth of the jar's soil, and figure a percentage for each component. [4]

■ TAKE THE PERCENTAGES to a nursery and discuss how to enrich your soil. Clay soil needs more air pores, created by adding lime, peat moss, sand, or wood ashes. Sandy soil needs its water drainage slowed down, and improves with humus, topsoil, or well-rotted manure. Silty soil holds extra moisture and gravel; manure mixed with straw or sand drains the excess.

CHAPTER SEVEN

The Art of Horticulture

Since no man knows the future,
who can tell him what is to come?
—ECCLESIASTES 8:7

A s an admirer of the French Impressionists' work, I've soaked in their sculptures and paintings at museums around the country while traveling for business and vacations. Impressionistic landscape paintings, created from Pontoise to Argenteuil, are as familiar to us as the calendars, wallpapers, and gift wrappings of today, but in nineteenth-century France, living and painting in the "open air" caused a stir. It just wasn't done in polite society.

However, as the French bourgeois began spending more time outdoors—hosting teas and boating parties, picnics and concerts, informal luncheons and gardening tours—landscape paintings flourished. When the painters Bazille, Caillebotte, Manet, Monet, Morisot, Pissarro, and Renoir captured the freshly blooming public parks and private gardens, they represented the cultural shifts of their era.

During this time horticulture emerged as a scientific as well as an artistic endeavor. A French publication in 1860 defined the word by printing this dialogue, almost as a gardening catechism:

Question: What is horticulture?

Answer: The art or means of making the best of any piece of land, be it from the standpoint of ornamentation or produce.

Question: What does the word horticulture mean?

I must admit the union of art and science in gardening has surprised and intrigued me.

Answer: It literally means "the cultivation of gardens" and comes from the Latin word *hortus*, meaning "garden," and the French word culture. Hence also the words horticulturists or gardeners, which we give to those who exercise the profession.

Question: Apart from agriculture and silviculture [forestry], has horticulture other points of contact with science, or is it independent of them?

Answer: It most certainly has. Horticulture itself . . . is but a part, a member of the great corpus of knowledge we designate by the name of natural sciences.[5]

Contrary to what I'd expect, the emphasis on gardening as a science didn't squelch the common person's burgeoning love for cultivating the land. In fact, the newborn "headiness" of science during this era enhanced the widespread interest in creating both utility (fruit and vegetable) and ornamental (plant and flower) gardens. A French gardening journal observed, "Fifty years ago nearly all farms limited their vegetable gardens to narrow plots, which were more often than not poorly cultivated, poorly kept up. Today farmers maintain gardens which are clean and properly cared for, rich in choice vegetables and strong, healthy fruit trees. Nor will you find these pretty little gardens, these orchards, these espaliers only among the well-to-do; you will find them among the poorest farmers as well." The author claimed that in addition to the appreciation of beauty, the people who cultivate these gardens "find a greater path to knowledge."[6]

Be it the influence of art or science, I'm grateful France looked to the future to understand about the earth's vegetation; this flurry of digging and planting birthed some of the most memorable paintings of all time and changed the direction of Western art. Impressionists painted everyday citizens, and increasingly, those people lived in and loved the garden.

However, I must admit the union of art and science in gardening has surprised and intrigued me. For most of my life, I've skirted science, judging it complex and boring, believing the artistic and systematic can't mix. Studying art history taught me otherwise, but so has nature. Unwittingly, I've learned the scientific means to keep flowers thriving while practicing the art of gardening.

At the same time, I'm relieved to discover myself still open to learning new things. As long as I breathe I want to be wholly alive, and the art of truly living depends on choosing adventure and pressing into the future. Aesthetic, scientific, or otherwise.

A Prayer for the Future

God, I resonate with the apostle Paul and proclaim, "Forgetting what is behind and straining toward what is ahead, I press on toward the goal to win the prize for which God has called me heavenward." In the garden, in my life, in whatever I do, I move ahead with You. Amen.

If we know God, we can emulate the French gardeners and embrace change. We can depend on the promise of Jeremiah 29:11-13: "'For I know the plans I have for you,' declares the LORD, 'plans to prosper you and not to harm you, plans to give you hope and a future. Then you will call upon me and come and pray to me, and I will listen to you. You will seek me and find me when you seek me with all your heart.'"

"Plants grow in response to their food intake," explains a soil-testing pamphlet in my office. "Certain types of food are obtained from air and water; others like [nutrients] are obtained from the soil. As plants grow, they deplete the soil of this life-giving food. When this supply is reduced below a certain level, soil needs fertilizer.

"However, if too many ingredients are added, plants become choked with food and react in the same way as if they did not have enough food. Testing your soil will allow you not only to avoid problems before they occur, but also to provide the right condition for the best possible growth."[7]

Some gardeners develop their own methods, but most buy a simple soil-testing kit at a local nursery or garden shop. The test indicates which nutrients need boosting and what fertilizers will replenish them. However, it helps to know that fertilizer packages boast three numbers, usually on the front, such as 5-10-5. In order, these numbers indicate the percentage of nitrogen, phosphorus, and potash or potassium (N, P, K) in the ingredients.

Each of the N, P, K ingredients plays a role in plant growth.

■ *Nitrogen.* A good supply of nitrogen aids dark-green foliage and guards against disease, infection, and injury.

■ *Phosphorus.* The presence of phosphorus produces plump seed germination, healthy seedlings, and vigorous flowers.

■ *Potash.* Stiff stalks and disease-resistant growth result from the appropriate amounts of potash.

An easy-to-use soil test will measure a garden plot's pH level, which is a measurement of its acidity (sourness) or alkalinity (sweetness) level, ranging from 1.0 to 14.0. A balanced condition is 7.0. The pH level indicates what N, P, K combination should be in the flower bed's fertilizer.

To eliminate the guesswork, take the pH level to a nursery and ask the professionals what fertilizer will boost the nutrients.[8]

CHAPTER EIGHT

An Ever-Expanding Vision

The vision is yet for the
appointed time.
—HABAKKUK 2:3, NASB

When Jenny Butchart decided to create a garden, her enterprising husband, Robert, considered his wife a visionary. If he hadn't thought this, she'd probably have been declared totally nuts, because Jenny wanted to grow flowers in a rock quarry.

That is the way of visionaries. Onlookers brand them as brilliant or befuddled, laudable or laughable, depending on their projects' outcome. Fortunately for the gardening world, Jenny's idea proved her a genius, and she possessed the plentiful resources to turn a hard-bitten pit into a floral masterpiece.

In 1888 Robert had left his dry-goods business to begin manufacturing cement near his Canadian birthplace in Ontario. By the century's end, his pioneering efforts had amassed a fortune in this new industry. Attracted to the West Coast because of its rich limestone deposits, he built a new factory at Tod Inlet on Vancouver Island and established a 130-acre family home there in 1904.

When Robert exhausted the limestone quarry near their house, Jenny conceived an unprecedented plan. Why not transform the scarred into the sacred? She requisitioned tons of topsoil from nearby farms, transported it by horse and cart, and lined the quarry's floor with fresh earth. Step by labored step, under her careful supervision the Butcharts' eyesore grew into a family heirloom and a community treasure. Jenny created a spectacular sunken garden, bursting with ravishing flowers and ornamental birds collected by her husband.

Why not transform the scarred into the sacred?

As also the case with visionaries, one successful idea led to another. Mirroring their worldwide travels, the Butcharts added a Japanese garden on the ocean side of their grounds, an Italian garden replaced their tennis court, and a rose garden supplanted a kitchen vegetable patch. By the 1920s more than fifty thousand visitors flooded to the estate each year, which the couple named "Benvenuto," the Italian word for "welcome."

Today only the chimney remains of Robert's cement factory kiln, but visitors still pour into the Butchart Gardens, a fifty-acre showplace owned by his descendants. Each year over one million plants of seven hundred varieties maintain the gardens' continuous bloom from March through October, contributing to its international reputation. That's approximately one visitor per planting, for nearly one million people pass through the gardens annually to enjoy its seasonal beauty and entertainment.[9]

Walking through the gardens' meandering paths a few years ago, I wondered about Jenny Butchart. *When she dreamed of reclaiming the used-up quarry, was she thinking only of the estate's appearance? Or did she envision the millions of visitors? Did she realize she'd created an ever-expanding vision, lasting for a century and beyond, passing to her daughters and later to the grandchildren?*

As I sipped tea and munched on finger sandwiches in the restaurant, I asked myself, *Did Jenny dream she'd provide a haven for life-weary travelers like me? A place to breathe in hope, dispelling the world's creeping despair?* Caught in a crisis at home, I'd escaped to Canada for a desperately needed vacation. As I crossed via ferry to Victoria, not knowing what waited across the waters, I'd prayed to find rest.

In a lovely inn I eventually found sleep and solitude, and from a brochure fatefully placed in the lobby, I discovered the Butchart legacy. For most of a day I soaked up Jenny's gardens and still-lingering hospitality. I stayed until the serenity seeped into my soul, and as I drove away from her beloved estate, I whispered to the gentle winds, "Thank you, Jenny, for your wonderful vision. Thank you for the gift of an enduring garden."

A Prayer for Vision

Lord, as I consider how to expand the garden, teach me about vision. Show me how to wait for it, prepare for it, and later share it with others. Use my vision to bless the world, as You have blessed me in the garden. Amen.

It's as innate as our bones to desire a vision for our lives, a path to follow with purpose, pleasure, and passion. But when God drops a vision into our hearts, it's never just to nourish and comfort ourselves. He intends for us to reflect His heart for the world, admonishing, blessing, comforting, and pointing lost souls to His Kingdom.

As the prophets and saints exemplified for us, vision exists for humanity's redemption. When we understand and live by this principle, we can rest assured that "the vision is yet for the appointed time. . . . Though it tarries, wait for it; for it will certainly come" (Habakkuk 2:3, NASB).

DIG, DIG, AND DOUBLE DIG

Especially when starting a perennial bed, many professional gardeners suggest tilling the soil in the fall, covering it with mulch, and waiting until spring to plant. It then expands and contracts with each winter freeze and thaw, breaking into smaller clumps and improving the structure.

Use these guidelines to break up ground for a garden.

▪ CHECK THE SOIL. To avoid destroying the soil's structure, it should be slightly moist before digging. If the soil feels sticky and forms a ball, it's too wet. If it crumbles into dust, it's too dry.

▪ OUTLINE THE PLOT. If it's a curved bed, use a garden hose to indicate the perimeter. If square or rectangular, mark the outer edge with stakes and a string.

▪ CUT THE EDGES. Using an edging tool, garden spade, or a straight-blade shovel, cut through the grass or vegetation, following the markers' pattern.

▪ REMOVE THE SOD. If grass grows within the potential flower bed, cut it in chunks, lift it out with a shovel, and use it to fill bare spots in the lawn. Or loosen the dirt and throw the grass into the compost.

▪ WORK THE GROUND. All across the bed, use a spade to lift up the soil, toss it forward, and break it apart with the blade. Avoid stepping on the broken soil so it won't compact.

▪ AMEND THE SOIL. Add compost, manure, peat moss, or other needed amendments.

For a deluxe treatment of the soil that superbly enhances plant life, try double digging the bed.

▪ DIG UP A TRENCH in a corner section of the bed. It should be about one-foot wide and as deep as a spade's blade.

▪ PLACE THE REMOVED SOIL aside in a cart or wheelbarrow.

▪ LOOSEN AND AMEND the trench's subsoil.

▪ DIG ANOTHER TRENCH next to the first one, transferring the topsoil from the second trench into the first trench.

▪ ADD AMENDMENTS to this topsoil, working it in thoroughly.

▪ REPEAT THE PROCEDURE for the entire bed.

▪ AMEND THE TOPSOIL from the first trench and place it in the last trench.[10]

HOW TO CREATE QUICK COLOR

As you dig up the ground, you also need to decide which flowers will appear in your newly plowed beds. Most gardeners use both annuals and perennials to create color in the garden. This selected list will help you decide which annuals to choose. There is also a list of biennials, which appear for two growing seasons. A selected list of perennials begins on page 82.

Remember that unlike perennials, annuals do not return to the garden year after year. However, they provide quick color and bloom all summer long, while perennials flower only for a few weeks. In some climates certain perennials may function as annuals, and vice versa. Annuals can also self sow, dropping seeds into the ground for new flowers in the next growing season.

ANNUALS		
Amaranth (Amaranthus)	18 inches to 6 feet	Full sun
Baby's-Breath	8 to 24 inches	Full sun
Balsam (Impatiens)	6 inches to 8 feet	Full sun to full shade
Bishop's Flower	2 to 3 feet	Full sun to partial shade
Candytuft	6 to 18 inches	Full sun
Cape Marigold	12 to 16 inches	Full sun
Celosia	6 to 24 inches	Full sun
China Aster	6 to 36 inches	Full sun to light shade
Chrysanthemum	1 to 3 feet	Full sun to partial shade
Cosmos	10 inches to 6 feet	Full sun to light shade
Creeping Zinnia	5 to 6 inches	Full sun
Dahlia	12 inches to 8 feet	Full sun
Everlasting	18 inches to 3 feet	Full sun
Flossflower	6 to 30 inches	Full sun
Geranium	10 to 36 inches	Full sun
Hawksbeard	8 to 18 inches	Full sun

Larkspur	1 to 4 feet	Full sun to light shade
Lobelia	4 to 8 inches	Full sun to partial shade
Marigold	6 inches to 3 feet	Full sun
Morning Glory	6 to 20 feet (vines)	Full sun
Nasturtium	6 inches to 8 feet	Full sun
Pansy	3 to 12 inches	Full sun to partial shade
Periwinkle	3 to 18 inches	Full sun to partial shade
Petunia	8 to 18 inches	Full sun
Phlox	6 to 20 inches	Full sun to partial shade
Pink	4 to 30 inches	Full sun to partial shade
Poppy	1 to 4 feet	Full sun to light shade
Pot Marigold	12 to 24 inches	Full sun
Safflower	1 to 3 feet	Full sun
Sage (Salvia)	8 inches to 4 feet	Full sun to partial shade
Snapdragon	6 inches to 4 feet	Full sun to partial shade
Sunflower	2 to 10 feet	Full sun
Wax Begonia	5 to 16 inches	Partial shade to shade
Yellow Ageratum	10 to 18 inches	Full sun
Zinnia	8 to 36 inches	Full sun

BIENNIALS

Bellflower	1 to 4 feet	Full sun to partial shade
Evening Primrose	2 to 8 feet	Full sun to partial shade
Forget-Me-Not	6 to 10 inches	Full sun to partial shade
Foxglove	2 to 6 feet	Partial shade
German Violet	8 to 24 inches	Partial to full shade
Hollyhock	2 to 9 feet	Full sun
Ornamental Cabbage	10 to 15 inches	Full sun
Statice, Sea Lavender	10 to 24 inches	Full sun [II]

CHAPTER NINE

Making Amends with the Earth

*How shall I make amends so that you
will bless the LORD's inheritance?*

—2 SAMUEL 21:3

A teenage niece passes through my sister's living room, and I'm caught in déjà vu for a moment. She's wearing a form-fitting shirt, a short skirt with tights, and a peace-symbol necklace.

"Oh, my, you're wearing the same stuff I did in high school," I observe with surprise and amusement.

After Kristy leaves, my sister explains, "Retro is really 'in' right now. The kids think it's cool."

"*Cool* was a word we used," I protest. "It was *our* expression. I suppose they're also into the peace and environmental stuff too? *Our* issues?"

"Yes."

"Well, that's actually good. Just so they know they weren't the *first* to think of it," I pronounce a bit too ardently and then laugh.

Lately I've been forced to admit that the ancient commentator was right: There is nothing new under the sun (Ecclesiastes 1:9). It's often just recycled and renamed.

I thought about this last week after a college-age environmentalist knocked on my door, soliciting funds for his organization and looking like a long-haired flashback to the late 1960s. I barely heard what he said. I kept thinking about how *young* he looked, how old that makes me, and how my college classmates and I wrestled with the same issues he does. Except we used the buzzword *ecology*.

Each new generation inherits an intensifying responsibility to make amends with the earth.

Later as I closed the door, I thought, *The more things change, the more they stay the same.* No matter what we call them, certain issues never disappear, and that's certainly true for our environment's deterioration. Each new generation inherits an intensifying responsibility to make amends with the earth.

In college I wrote a zealous freshman term paper about ecological responsibility, borrowing heavily from Francis Schaeffer, a popular theologian of the time. He wrote, "[We are] to honor what God has made, up to the very highest level that [we] can honor it, without sacrificing [humanity. We] should not be the destroyers. We should treat nature with an overwhelming respect."[12]

Typing at the desk in my dorm room, I earnestly intended to respect the environment, but when career pressures ensued, my resolve melted away. It's not that I trashed the earth; I just didn't think much about it. But once again horticulture— growing intimate with nature and observing its ways—redirected my attention. As unpredictable seasons, with no discernible beginning or end, and disruptive weather patterns foiled my gardening plans, the punctured ozone became a reality to me. As I noticed fewer earthworms in a certain flower bed, I wondered about species becoming instinct. As I fed the shrubs in the yard, I quit thinking of them merely as ornamentation. A gardening book had reminded me that I need their oxygen.

I'm not demonstrative in public, so even with my renewed interest in nature, it's improbable that I'll ram a whaling boat or chain myself to a tree for the environment's sake. Yet in simple ways I can revive my forgotten goal and make amends with the earth. I can recycle. Build a compost pile. Use environmentally safe pesticides. Buy pump rather than spray can products. Nourish the soil and the organisms that call it home. In many seemingly small ways I can choose to garden organically, returning the earth's products, once they're used up and disposable, back to the ground to replenish it.

Most of all, I can remember this principle. If there is nothing new under the sun—no new earth or ecosystem or atmosphere or other elements that form the environment—it's wise to cherish what's already here and preserve it for future generations.

Indeed, some things never change, and spiritually this can be good news. God told the Israelites, "I the LORD do not change. So you, O descendants of Jacob, are not destroyed" (Malachi 3:6). Despite their spiritual waywardness, God still loved His people with an unshakable love. He did not revoke His promises to them.

Nor does He forget His words to us. "Your kingdom is an everlasting kingdom, and your dominion endures through all generations," wrote the psalmist. "The LORD is faithful to all his promises and loving toward all he has made" (Psalm 145:13).

A Prayer of Remembrance

Lord, thank You for the great gift of the earth. With Your help, I will remember to honor Your creation, doing what I can to preserve it for the generations to come. I will respect the environment in remembrance of You and Your faithfulness to us. Amen.

THE ABCs OF AMENDMENTS

Amendments are "bulky, usually porous, materials, either organic or mineral. Worked into the soil, they enhance aeration, drainage, and microscopic life, enabling the soil to better hold nutrients and the optimal amount of water."[13]

Mineral amendments such as sand and lime, though needed to improve certain soils, tend to leach away with time. Organic amendments are those derived from plant or animal materials. They break down and turn into humus, which makes the soil porous and crumbly, easier to manage, and a better place for plants.

In simplified terms, these are the ABCs of soil amendments.

- ASK what the soil needs. Test the soil for its composition and needed amendments.

- BUY the appropriate amendments at nurseries or gardening shops, or in some cases such as compost, create it in the backyard.

- CULTIVATE the soil by thoroughly mixing in the amendments.

The following are dependable organic and mineral soil amendments that can be purchased in bags and sometimes in bulk.

- COMPOST. Used to improve soil, fertilize, or mulch. Purchased in bags or bulk or made from garden wastes and kitchen scraps.

- GROUND BARK. A long-lasting amendment of tree bark, such as fir or pine, that improves soil structure. Needs to be blended well into the soil.

- LEAF MOLD. Decomposed leaves used to add nutrients and improve structure. Good for acid-loving plants. Don't use leaves from walnut trees, which are toxic to plants.

- LIME. Raises the pH level of acid soil, loosens clay soil, and increases nutrient-holding capacity.

- MANURE. Good conditioner with slight amounts of nitrogen, phosphorus, and potassium.

- PEAT MOSS. Helps soil retain water. If used with another amendment, wet and mix thoroughly before adding to the soil.

- SAND. Improves drainage of clay soil. Use only coarse sand, not beach sand or the kind used on icy roads. They contain salt.[14]

CHAPTER TEN

The Magic of a Good Wait

Wait for the LORD; be strong and take heart and wait for the LORD.

—PSALM 27:14

Today I set stiff goals for writing more entries in this book, so naturally I wound up puttering in my flower gardens. (A prolific author once told me he works on five books at a time so he can always procrastinate on four!) But casting aside a writer's bent toward delaying her work, what draws me to the flower beds?

Along with dirt diggers through the ages, I espouse the joys of getting close to the earth and respecting its rhythms. On my more philosophical days, I think of myself as participating in an ancient ritual of tending the earth on God's behalf. My mind floats to multitudes of people before me who followed their instincts to create and nurture—and fell captive to the mystical sights and smells of the flower garden. These romantic musings, however, don't negate the fact that gardening requires dirty work and often insists that I wait for results.

Actually, I should be surprised that I'm a gardener, because most of my life I've been lured by the siren of instant gratification. My sister claims that as a newborn I popped out of the womb wanting things my way, right away. I resist her description of me as the spoiled, youngest child, yet I know that personally and professionally I've chosen short-term activities and writing projects that produce quick gratification. I recognize that this sister speaks a kernel of truth.

Gardening, then, marked a transition of outlook and character for me. Planting a row of peonies four years ago meant waiting until this summer for fullness and blooms. It took three years for the hostas to reach the size I'd hoped for, and I don't know if the lilacs will ever resemble the sweet-smelling bushes of my youth. When I divided the irises one fall, they skipped a spring before blooming again, and after replanting them a few times, the chives now arrive in late winter on their own. I've read that a hundred years pass before a garden fully matures, and that's probably why the daylilies and roses near the house perform faithfully, whether or not I've tended them. This house is over a century old, and these perennial bloomers are "up in years" too.

I could feel discouraged by this one-hundred-year principle, but I choose not to. Even though the earth takes its time, I can still reap rewards in my small back-yard plots. And in light of a century, waiting a year or two for the bleeding hearts to double in size doesn't seem so bad. In the end it's the hope of plenty that sustains me through the preparatory or dormant months when I'm either burying things in the ground or cutting them back and when sweaty work yields no perceptible outcome except sore muscles and an aching back. Even I—the writer of all things short—accept that in the garden there is no instant anything.

On the other hand, there is magic in "a good wait." In nature there dwells a cyclical pattern of dying to eventually spring back with new life. In the fall I cut down, cover up,

Along with dirt diggers of the ages, I espouse the joys of getting close to the earth and respecting its rhythms.

and abandon the flower beds. Strolling across the yard in December, examining where flowers used to burgeon and cascade, it seems doubtful they'll ever bloom again. Yet the following July the yard crowds with color, if I exercise faith and perseverance during the months between. The same is true when I plant seeds and young flowers in the spring. I nestle them into the ground, and they don't look like much, but if I allow nature to "take its course," later they entertain me with sprouts and blooms.

I just have to wait.

This notion isn't original, but as I've worked in the yard, I've thought of how the delayed-gratification principle of gardening relates to the fulfillment of our desires.

Jesus said that unless a grain of wheat falls to the ground and dies, it will never yield a harvest (John 12:24). So it is with unmet expectations. Before fulfilling our dreams, God often cuts down and buries them in a character-development process that feels like death. Then later when we're content to live without them, He resurrects those desires and hands them to us. They're more beautiful and bountiful than we'd imagined, and we realize they're a product of the difficult times of a winter past.

"I am still confident of this: I will see the goodness of the LORD in the land of the living," wrote the psalmist on behalf of us all (Psalm 27:13).

We just have to wait.

A Waiting Prayer

Lord, teach me to wait for the work of the garden, believing that sowing begets reaping, that each burial holds the promise of resurrection. As I wait for nature to sprout and bloom, I'll remember to wait patiently for You to work in my life too. Amen.

The necessity of "a good wait" certainly applies to compost, a soil amendment that improves the earth's structure but takes time to become the finished product.

Compost can be purchased in prepackaged bags at nurseries, but many homemade versions abound, allowing gardeners to recycle leftovers from the lawn and kitchen.

"Consisting mainly of partially decayed plant wastes, it is an excellent source of organic matter and a reservoir for many nutrients," say the experts. "As an amendment, compost can convert a sandy or clayey soil into loam [good soil]. As a fertilizer, finished compost provides a good balance of two parts nitrogen to one part each of phosphorus and potassium. If it is made from a large variety of materials, compost will obtain a healthy balance of trace elements as well as the major nutrients."[15]

To make compost, gardeners combine two types of plant materials: the "browns," which are fibrous materials such as leaves, straw, and sawdust, and the "greens" derived from lawn clippings and food scraps. The browns and greens are placed alternately in a pile or bin, kept as moist as a well-squeezed sponge, and turned regularly to incorporate air.

The material present in this "hot composting" method shrinks to about one-third of its original size and can be ready in as little as a month. "Cold composting" is less work because the pile remains undisturbed, but takes up to two years for the material to decompose and be ready for the garden.

Materials for composting include: autumn leaves, twigs, perennial tops; by-products from crops; coffee grounds; discarded bulbs; eggshells; fallen fruit; farm animal manure; fruit and vegetable scraps; grass clippings; sawdust and shavings; sod; straw; used mulch (chips and hay); wood ashes.

Fish are good, if buried deep in the pile so animals don't smell them.

"Thick scraps" such as corncobs and melon or grapefruit rinds decompose slowly.[16]

Creative Groundwork

PLANTING WITH A FULL HEART AND HANDS

May the favor of the Lord our God rest upon us;
establish the work of our hands for us—
yes, establish the work of our hands.

—PSALM 90:17

CHAPTER ELEVEN

The Work of Our Hands

Do whatever your hand finds to do,
for God is with you.

—1 Samuel 10:7

My father had "a thing" about tools. All kinds of tools.

Dad owned hand tools for the garden, gas-propelled tools for the lawn, electric power tools for the house, and a huge collection of tools for car repair and maintenance. When he died two decades ago, the biggest decision about his personal possessions was, "Who will get the tools?" I still lovingly use a couple of his hammers and screwdrivers and wish I'd taken more, because Dad's tools were sacred.

Dad's tools also invoked fear, if we were caught using the ones he reserved, usually locked up in a metal box, for himself. "Who took my good hammer?" he'd half ask, half complain through the house. "You guys (Midwestern term for everyone in the family) aren't supposed to mess with my good tools," he'd add with frustration, as if a tool's character could be good or bad. Only God could comfort the person who'd used that hammer because according to Dad, we'd probably messed it up or at least not handled it properly. (Never mind that *he* could leave them greasy and abandoned on the garage floor.)

Aside from "borrowing" a hammer or shovel, I never considered myself interested in, let alone obsessed with, tools. Then years later I began gardening, and it didn't take long to prove I was definitely my father's daughter. Encountering implements hanging jauntily on garden shop walls, I learned that according to professional gardeners, a multi-purpose shovel didn't exist. Their handles were short or long, skinny or thick, with variations on straight or curved blades, depending on whether I wanted to turn over soil, dig a hole for a post, or cut edges along flower beds. Spades and trowels were skinny, medium, and wide, based on the desire to plant, transplant, or merely scoop soil. There were small hand rakes, skinny bed-cleaning rakes, steel soil-penetrating rakes, and plastic leaf-gathering rakes. The rows of implements seemed to stretch endlessly, and for most tools I could select from an array of woods, plastics, metals, colors, styles, designs, and trademarks.

After visiting several shops I couldn't decide which tools to choose. Like my father before me, I simply wanted them all.

After visiting several shops I couldn't decide which tools to choose. Like my father before me, I simply wanted them all. Unfortunately, having them all didn't fit my budget, and that meant creating personal guidelines for purchasing and caring for tools, such as:

■ *Choose the tool that manages as many tasks as possible.* Generally, one trowel, one shovel, one pruner can accomplish several tasks.

■ *Buy the best the budget allows,* but this doesn't necessitate purchasing top-of-the-line items. Sturdy, middle-priced tools can endure.

■ *Care for tools and they'll last longer.* Clean them after use, and periodically apply a light oil to the blades (WD-40 or something similar) and wood cleaner to the handles. Dry thoroughly so they won't rust. Sharpen blades as needed.

■ *Think twice* about whether it's needed. I have specialty tools that sit in a basket, while I repeatedly use the basic versions. The "old standbys" usually work best.

These guidelines have reigned me in, but I still salivate when the latest gardening catalog arrives in the mail. A recent issue displays six sizes of pruners, several kinds of shears, various hose guides, and a set of bedding tools I didn't know existed. I placate myself by listing on the order form anything I desire—and then toss it in the wastebasket. Somehow *pretending* I can buy everything at once satisfies me.

In the meantime, I remember that my existing tools are dirty, pull them out for cleaning, and fondly remember Dad.

I think tools are important because they extend the work of our hands, and God intends for us to profit from our work. If we're doing what He designed us to do, our benefits are obvious. We can profit mentally, emotionally, physically, financially. But God also benefits from putting our hands to work.

When God called Moses to deliver His people from the Egyptians, the Lord said to him, "What is that in your hand?" (Exodus 4:2). Moses replied, "A staff," and God used that "tool" to set captives free. Likewise, when the Lord asks us to accomplish a task for His kingdom, He frequently uses the "tool" in our hands—the thing we already love and know how to do.

Whether we employ our hands to teach or write or preach or repair or garden, if we're using them according to His calling, we glorify the Lord and point seekers to Him.

A Blessing for the Hands

Lord, as I work in the garden, please bless the work of my hands. May the time I spend digging and planting be pleasing to You. May it bless Your name and extol the mighty hand that created and watches over the earth. Amen.

BASIC TOOLS FOR THE TRADE

For a person with few or no tools, these items ensure a good start for tending new or established flower beds. (See page 126 for adding to this basic list.)

■ BUSHEL BASKET. Toss in leaves, weeds, and other discards, and transport them to the trash.

■ BEDDING RAKE. Short- or long-handled, this narrow rake reaches between flowers to clean debris-filled beds.

■ EDGING TOOL. This tool evenly slices the ground, creating edges for beds.

■ FLOWER/GRASS SHEARS. Garden shears snip dead blooms and leaves, plus unwieldy grass.

■ FLOWER SHOVEL. It cultivates close to the plants without clobbering them. Look for a shorter-length handle and an almost heart-shaped blade.

■ GARDEN HOE. Available in several sizes, a garden hoe chops weeds and moves soil around.

■ GARDEN HOSE. One hose or several connected together reach and water flower beds. Rubber hoses move and wind the easiest.

■ HAND CULTIVATOR. A cultivator loosens the soil in new or existing flower beds.

■ HAND FORK. For breaking up topsoil and transplanting, a hand fork sports three or more straight or slightly bent tines.

■ HAND WEEDER. The angled, sharp blade hacks weeds efficiently.

■ KNIFE/PRUNER. A basic knife or pruner pierces, cuts, and pries into dirt and plants. Choose a straight design with a serrated blade.

■ LONG-HANDLED SPADE. A rectangular-shaped blade digs "holes" with straight sides, creates edging, or pulls up plants.

■ MULTI-GALLON BUCKET. Used to haul water, fertilizer, and other liquids, buckets are commonly made of rubber or steel.

■ SOIL RAKE. The steel teeth of a soil rake penetrate and break up compacted earth. Flipped over, the rake grades and smoothes soil.

■ TROWEL. The multiuse trowel usually digs holes to plant and transplant, and is available in several blade widths.

■ WAGON/WHEELBARROW. A child's wagon or a lightweight wheelbarrow carts flowers and fertilizer, tools and equipment.

CHAPTER TWELVE

In Praise of Seeds

As... a garden causes seeds to grow, so the Sovereign
LORD will make righteousness and praise spring up.

—ISAIAH 61:11

F or all the wonderful things in the wonderful universe of God, nothing seems to me more sur-
prising than the planting of a seed in the blank earth and the result thereof. Take the Poppy seed,
for instance: it lies in your palm the merest atom of matter, hardly visible, a speck, a pin's point
in bulk, but within it is imprisoned a spirit of beauty ineffable, which will break its bonds and
emerge from the dark ground and blossom in a splendor so dazzling as to baffle all powers of description.

The Genie in the Arabian tale isn't half so astonishing. In this tiny casket lie folded roots, stalks,
leaves, buds, flowers, seed-vessels,—surpassing color and beautiful form, all that goes to make up a plant
which is as gigantic in proportion to the bounds that confine it as the Oak is to the acorn. You may watch
this marvel from beginning to end in a few weeks' time, and if you realize how great a marvel it is, you
can but be lost in "wonder, love, and praise." . . . But if I were to pause on the threshold of the year to
consider the miracles of seeds alone, I should never, I fear, reach my garden plot at all.[1]

—CELIA THAXTER, *AN ISLAND GARDEN*, 1894

Poets and gardeners, songwriters and scientists all agree: A seed is a miracle.

"A seed, like a hen's egg, contains everything necessary to create a new life," explains professional gardener Susan McClure.[2] "There is an embryo of a baby plant, stored food, and a seed coat that binds it all in a neat package." When buried in the soil and nourished with light and water, one seed can sprout abundant delphinium blooms, a fleshy orbed pumpkin, a woody stemmed azalea bush, or a gigantic centurial redwood.

Every spring when I discover unexpected weeds and flowers in surprising places, nature admonishes me.

I agree with the poet Celia Thaxter that the "Genie in the Arabian tale isn't half so astonishing" as a seed, especially when considering a plant's ability to reproduce itself, by itself. In the appropriate season seeds drop to the ground, poised to travel the wind's back to an undisclosed location where they snuggle in, take root, and astonish us with stems and leaves and blooms. Every spring when I discover unexpected weeds and flowers in surprising places, nature admonishes me. "Even without your help, we do quite well, thank you," say the unidentified plants smiling up at me. And I am forced to agree.

Of course, human hands still help and hasten the sowing process. One of my favorite paintings is *Sower* (1850) by Jean-Francois Millet, which depicts a lone French peasant, backdropped by the rising sun, scattering seeds with the sweep of his powerful arm. He strides heartily across the newly plowed field, evoking the icons of my Willa Cather and cornhusking Nebraska youth. (Though I grew up in the city, pioneer images still seeped within.) The sower reminds me of our elemental relationship to and dependence on the earth.

Both fortunately and unfortunately in recent decades we've sanitized, categorized, manipulated, and mechanized the ancient art of sowing into a mass produced, barely recognizable form of its simple self. This is fortunate because we're able to feed millions of hungry people around the world, and I would never spurn this ability. But in the midst of the noisy machinery and endless organization, we've lost our basic hand-to-plow connection to the earth and its Maker.

Even the backyard flower gardener can lose this connection, making the process more complicated and expensive than necessary. My gardening catalogs urge me to purchase germinating and transplanting mixes, propagation systems and grow lights, thermometers and fans, watering wands and humidity trays, heat mats and timers. All of these appeal to me, but I need to remind myself that our grandmothers and grandfathers planted seeds in empty eggshells or cartons and grew them in window sills. Or they waited until spring and dropped seeds in the ground, one by one.

Their unadorned sowing methods remind me of my earthly roots—and that the "old ways" are still good ways to nurture the spirit.

Prayer for Sowing Seeds

Lord, just as seeds need time to sprout and grow, so I need time to change and grow personally. Help me to be patient with this process, remembering that Your love and understanding don't end. Plant the seeds of endurance in me. Amen.

If we ask God to usher change into our lives—especially when we want to alter something about ourselves—we can remember the act of seed planting. Though we prefer the quick and supposedly painless process inherent in the latest fad, choosing this route to personal and spiritual transformation produces spindly, disheartening results.

On the other hand, if we carefully dig within and let God plant His seeds of change inside us, over time we'll grow personally healthy and spiritually strong. We "will be called oaks of righteousness, a planting of the LORD for the display of his splendor" (Isaiah 61:3).

Since I'm not a gardener who grows much from seeds, I'll depend on the experts from the *Treasury of Gardening* for seed-planting guidance. The following is their advice. Also check the information on the back of seed packets.

■ PREPARING A SEEDBED. "A seedbed should be raked smooth and have all dirt clumps broken so that a fine, even surface is formed. Mark rows with tautly pulled string between the stakes, then dig shallow furrows using the side of a trowel or a thick board. Use the string as a guide. Furrows should be about three times the size of the seed planted."

■ SOWING THE SEEDS. "Drop individual seeds into the furrows, spacing them 1/4 to 1/2 inch apart. Cover them with very fine, sifted soil or with seed starting mix purchased from a garden supplier. Cover the seeds to a depth of two to three times their diameter."

■ WATERING THE SEEDBED. "Check the seedbed several times a day, spraying the seeds with a fine water spray to keep the soil moist but not soaked."

■ THINNING THE SEEDLINGS. "When the seedlings reach the stage where they have the second set of true leaves . . . thin them by pulling out the extra seedlings so they're spaced two inches apart."

■ STARTING IN PEAT POTS. "As an alternative to starting seeds directly in an outdoor seedbed, it's possible to start them in peat pots or packs [indoors or outside]. Plant two or three seeds per individual cube, then thin to the sturdiest one when the seedlings are at the proper stage."

■ USING GROW LAMPS. "Seeds can be started during any season if they are grown indoors under grow lamps. They need between 16 to 18 hours a day." Seeds can also be started in sunny window sills.

■ HARDENING OFF SEEDLINGS. "Potted or boxed seedlings should be hardened off for a week or so before transplanting into the garden. Carry them outside and leave them there for a longer time each day before bringing them in overnight. This will wean them away from the indoor, hothouselike growing conditions without setting them back from shock."[3]

CHAPTER THIRTEEN

The Joy of a Good Buy

Out of her earnings she plants a vineyard.
—PROVERBS 31:16

he really BIG sale! Perennials, trees, shrubs, evergreens. Remember we hold nothing for nobody. This is one serious plant acquisition competition.

This warning about a Labor Day weekend sale greeted me as I opened the newsletter from Los Robles, my unquestionably favorite nursery in town. The newsletter's logo is accompanied by the tag line, "for information, inspiration, and perspiration," and it capsulizes the reasons I love shopping at this place filled with colorful plants and people.

I stumbled upon the nursery several years ago. Driving to the grocery store I spotted a small sign with the words "Los Robles" and an arrow pointing north, posted on a telephone pole. Impulsively I turned my car to the right, headed down an obscure side street, and ever since have faithfully forked over money to Christina and her gang. Christina is the nursery's owner, and the ambiance she creates naturally captures gardeners' hearts and loyalty.

Entering Los Robles for the first time, by the shop's door rather than the nursery's gate, I immediately resonated with its style. Quality gardening tools, gadgets, and ornaments crammed onto every shelf, wall, and floor space. Here were the cherub statues, the fabulous watering cans, the artistic pots and birdhouses I thought I'd never find. Venturing into the attached greenhouse, full of plants and more pots and topiaries and surprises, I submerged into the mesmerizing sights and smells and pinched myself. *Could I be Alice in Wonderland? Maybe so,* I thought, as the resident cat crept by and disappeared.

I had to see more—and definitely buy something.

Outdoors I discovered the largest and most varied selection of healthy annuals and perennials I'd witnessed to date. Sprawling herbs beckoned from one greenhouse, while another many-windowed building, devoted to shade plants, prophesied the end of my worries about a sun-deprived backyard. Yet for all its quality and style and abundance, the most appealing aspect of Los Robles's mystique emerged from its whimsical touch. It emanated from footed flower pots, the creative signs, the childlike red wagons for piling up purchases, the homemade newsletter, but most of all from Christina.

When Christina works the cash registers or passes me on the grounds, I wind up laughing or at least smiling broadly. Once when I bought some potted impatiens in August, she punched the numbers into her cash register and surmised, "Your mother must be coming to visit, huh?"

How did she know? I haven't a clue. But that is one of the wonders of Christina. She contributes something unexpected to the joy of a good buy.

Last year Christina lost her lease and for several months couldn't find a suitable location to rent. Then with no breath to spare, she moved into a large, flat lot across town, just in time for the spring buying season. I reluctantly admit, however, that on my first

That is one of the wonders of Christina. She contributes something unexpected to the joy of a good buy.

visit I didn't like the new setting. It lacked the nook-and-cranny charm, the cozy squeezing around corners, and the shaded comfort of overhead trees, roofs, and trellises. Except for the shop and greenhouses, Los Robles now spreads across a shadeless acreage that's terribly hot in our merciless Julys. But the new grounds won't sway my loyalty because the products and people remain reassuringly the same. Especially Christina, who over a few years will weave magic into this place too.

In the meantime, Christina herself is the entertainment. On my last visit it was so hot she walked around the shop spritzing herself with water from a spray bottle to cool off. I trudged toward the cash register, about to drop from the heat. When I reached the counter, she said, "Would you like for me to take care of you?" I thought she wanted to total my purchases, and I said yes. Then she sprayed me in the face with water. How could I not appreciate a shopkeeper as thoughtful as that?

Just as we revel in the joy of a good buy, we can reap the gladness of making good personal choices. Look around. People who live in peace, not regretful of the past or afraid of the future, are those who've consistently chosen to live according to God's values. They are like the wise and hard-working woman in Proverbs: "She is clothed with strength and dignity; she can laugh at the days to come. She speaks with wisdom, and faithful instruction is on her tongue" (Proverbs 31:25-26).

"To laugh at the days to come" is to have lived wisely. And to live wisely is to choose, day by day, to walk in God's way.

Many gardeners skip seed sowing and purchase young plants and flowers that have been grown in greenhouses and hardened off for a new life in the earth. To delight in the joy of a good buy, try these suggestions for local shopping.

▪ CREATE A PLAN. Before leaving the house, list the specific plants and the number of each you want to buy. Caught in a springtime shopping frenzy, it's easy to forget what or how many flowers the garden needs.

▪ SET A BUDGET. Sorting through the many and unexpected "good buys" in a place, it's easy to overspend. However, leave room in the budget for unexpected, must-have purchases.

▪ VISIT THE EXPERTS. Professional gardeners offer healthy plants, sometimes with a guarantee, and reliable advice. Nurseries are the best place to shop, and usually the flower selection is replenished into the summer.

If nurseries seem too high priced, then try gardening shops or even grocery stores, if you shop early in the season. These plants are less dependable so inspect them carefully. Also, supplies run out fast.

▪ INSPECT THE PLANTS. Insist on rich green leaves, blooms without brown spots and edges, a sturdy stalk. Check under the leaves and in the potting soil for tiny bugs. If a plant isn't healthy and insect free when it leaves the shop, it may struggle in the yard and infect the flowers near it.

▪ READ THE GUIDELINES. Can the yard live up to the size, sunlight, and watering requirements for a plant? Ask the nursery professionals about unfamiliar plants. Are they easy to care for? What conditions do they prefer?

▪ WAIT FOR SALES. If you're willing to spread out planting time, you can save money by shopping the sales toward the end of June. Also, don't miss the end-of-summer price reductions. The fall is a good time to plant trees, shrubs, roses, and perennials.

▪ SWAP WITH GARDENERS. Ask friends and neighbors for cuttings from their plants or castoffs when they thin out seedlings or divide perennials. Offer them the same.

CHAPTER FOURTEEN

There Is a Season

*There is a time for everything, and a
season for every activity under heaven.*

—ECCLESIASTES 3:1

I almost missed planting my garden this year.

During May and June my writing deadlines collided with a thin pocketbook, and while I sat in the house pounding on computer keys, I paused for rueful looks into the neglected backyard. From my office window I noticed stalks of grass shooting up among the bleeding heart blooms, the bare spots in the shade garden, and trees I should have pruned in the early spring.

"Now this is an irony," I lamented to myself. "Because I'm writing a gardening book, I don't have time to garden." I thought of past summers and how I'd spent entire days in the yard, until darkness descended. Especially during planting season, I'd turned childlike in my focus, forgetting to eat lunch, waiting until the last possible moment to head for the bathroom, and refusing to go inside when the streetlights came on. I was too busy planting and playing.

So after days of feeling sorry for myself, I decided that at least for this year, I'd redefine how I managed a planting season. It finally dawned on me that resurrecting the flower beds needn't be an all-or-nothing event, though my personality wants to operate that way. Instead of spending endless hours in the yard, I'd sneak away from my writing for short stints of weed pulling and transplanting. Rather than exhausting myself to finish everything by Memorial Day weekend, I'd extend my planting time into June. And because my financial resources are more limited than years past, I wouldn't plant every patch and pot and window box. *Better to "plant small" than nothing at all,* I thought.

Eventually we make our way back to the earth, where we discover that during our time away, the garden patiently waited for us.

Several years ago when I started my garden, an employee at a nursery said to me, "You know, everybody is in such a hurry to plant everything in May. I like to be more leisurely about my planting, taking time to enjoy it, so you'll find me still planting in June." As she packed up my herb purchases I thought, *She's missing out on growing time for her flowers.* But now I understood. *Better to plant late than not at all.*

Interestingly, my delayed-planting scheme paid off in ways I didn't expect. In June a friend gave me money "to spend on something fun," so I bought flowers. By then my perennials, several years old now, had grown back bigger than I'd anticipated. This meant I only needed a few annuals to fill in that bed. Later, when I took my modest allowance to a nursery, its value doubled because annuals were on sale for half price. I also found large but reasonably priced herbs, so when I planted them in late June, it looked as though they'd been in the ground for a month. What a wonderful serendipity! Waiting to plant actually had rewarded me financially.

After finishing my planting season in early July, I explained to my neighbor Susie why I'd scaled down my work on the garden this year. "I'm writing a gardening book and can't devote much time in the garden, nor do I have much money to spend," I admitted. "I wonder what my readers would think of that."

"Tell them that sometimes life gets in the way of gardening," she answered immediately, "and not to worry when it does."

Susie is wise and pragmatic. She is also right. As with the garden, our lives are seasonal. There are times of love and leisure, when we can lavish attention on the garden or simply enjoy its sensations. There are also seasons of stress and setbacks, when nature takes its own course without us. We simply don't have the resources—time, energy, or finances—to work much in the garden. But as Susie says, we need not fret. Seasons change, and eventually we make our way back to the earth, where we discover that during our time away, the garden patiently waited for us.

Perhaps more than we do, the garden understands that for everything there is a season.

When we're impatient with our circumstances, we can remember that throughout our lives, we pass through seasons. What feels endless and untenable often is a passing time that God uses to train us for better things ahead. We must remember that in the earth and in our lives, He is the God of new seasons.

King Solomon understood this characteristic of our Maker and explained, "There is a time for everything, and a season for every activity under heaven . . . . [God] has made everything beautiful in its time" (Ecclesiastes 3:1, 11).

A Prayer for Planting

Lord, I plant young flowers in the ground, eager for them to grow. Thank You for this remarkable ritual of nurture and anticipation. It reminds me that like springtime in the garden, there are seasons when You plant deeply in me too. Help me to be patient with Your seasons for my life, recognizing their value and needfulness. Amen.

PLANT, PLANT, AND TRANSPLANT

There is a season for planting, and it's filled with the joy of anticipation. Here's how to place bedding plants in the ground.

■ CHECK THE WEATHER. Try to plant on a partly cloudy day with no wind. If this isn't possible, plant in the early morning or evening when the weather has cooled off. Avoid planting in hot temperatures so the flowers won't wilt severely.

If you must plant in the heat or wind, cover the flowers with protective shields (commercial plant protectors or newspaper sheets) for about two days.

■ CHECK THE GROUND. Avoid planting in a flower bed that's soggy or dry. Slightly moist, crumbly soil is ideal for planting.

■ WATER THOROUGHLY.
While the plant is still in its container, water it thoroughly. This will help it slip out easily.

■ DIG A GENEROUS HOLE. It should be slightly deeper and wider than the plant's container.

■ TURN OVER THE POT. Tap the bottom and the plant should slip out into your hand. If it doesn't, massage the container slightly. Don't pull the plant out by its stem or rip the roots. The plant should be pulled out intact with only a few tiny roots left behind.

If the plant still won't budge, carefully snip away a bit of the plastic container, without cutting the roots, and let it gently fall out.

■ PLANT THE HOLE. There is no need to break away the container soil around the plant's root system, though some may fall away after leaving the container. Place the plant, container soil and all, in the hole. The top of the container soil should be even or slightly lower than the ground. With your fingers, pack the soil gently around the plant.

■ WATER AGAIN. Water the new plantings thoroughly, preferably with a root starter solution, a liquid fertilizer, or watered-down, well-rotted manure.

■ BE PATIENT. Freshly planted flowers tend to wilt a bit before they "take hold" in their new surroundings. With the proper water and sunlight, in a day or two they'll perk up. And don't worry: a plant that grows too big for its location can always be transplanted.

CHAPTER FIFTEEN

The Immutable Laws of Jekyll

I the LORD do not change.
— MALACHI 3:6

Pure idleness seems to me to be akin to folly. I must obey the Divine command: 'Work while ye have the light.'" This was the pragmatic work ethic of the irrepressible English gardener Gertrude Jekyll, who at the turn of the century revolutionized the Victorian garden with the stab of a trowel.

Gertrude contained such immense talents she *had* to work. Either that or implode. Before she took up gardening as a profession, a friend said, "There is hardly any useful handicraft the mysteries of which she has not mastered—carving, modeling, house-painting, carpentry, smith's work, repoussé work, gilding, wood-inlaying, embroidery, gardening, and all manner of herb and flower culture."[4] Gertrude was also an accomplished potter, photographer, and watercolorist.

A constant source of ideas and energy, Gertrude infused excellence into whatever she did. So it probably surprised no one that at midlife she parlayed her creativity and intelligence into an international career as a horticulturist. In the last half of her life Gertrude wrote sixteen books and 1,032 articles about gardening. According to her biographer, "She ran her nursery, took photographs for all her books, and carried out about 250 private garden and planting design commissions."[5] As if that wasn't enough, she also completed another 120 commissions with the landscape architect Edwin Lutyens, who fondly called her "Aunt Bumps."

Though Gertrude's world swirled with the change of ideas and projects, she held to her own immutable laws of garden design. Not fame, nor insistent clients, nor the lure of modern culture crumbled her foundational principles, and eventually they established an enduring reverence for her work. "For all its rigor, the Jekyll style, too, was born of affection—her love for the simple English cottage gardens she thought unsurpassed in their use of color and form," says the garden writer Ethne Clark, who explains Gertrude's predominant principles.

Gertrude wanted clients to feel the same warmth, the same awesome wonder, as she did while gazing at the garden.

- *Color coordination.* "She manipulated the rules of color association to create specific effects in her gardens. She frequently planted a herbaceous border with colors from the warm end of the spectrum at the middle, fading off to silver, cream, pink, mauve, and silver blue at the ends, so that one's eye was stimulated and then refreshed as one passed along the length of the border."

- *Design details.* She also gave "critical attention to the details of the design. A Gertrude Jekyll-style garden is a design totality; the garden is an extension of the house, and as much thought, energy, and expense is spent on furnishing the garden as on the house. The materials, design, and function of an item were all chosen for their appropriateness to a vernacular garden setting."

- *Planned progression.* Gertrude planned her gardens for a progression of flowering plants. "Jekyll went to extraordinary lengths to keep her gardens in flower: pot-grown lilies were plunged into gaps left by fading perennials; early annuals were bedded out to cover the ground between later-season perennials."[6]

Gertrude's typical gardens required constant care, and most of us can't afford the time and expense of her adventures. Yet if we'll look closely at the modest but satisfying gardens around us, we'll find Aunt Bumps's unchangeable principles still at work. Basic "ground rules" for garden planting earn their status because whether they're applied to an apartment plot or a grand estate, they produce memorable viewpoints.

Maybe that's why Gertrude remained so staunch. She wanted clients to feel the same warmth, the same awesome wonder, as she did while gazing at a garden. A landscape architect who knew Gertrude wrote about the vitality in her face. It reflected the gratification of gardening.

In His own determined way, God has created unalterable rules for living. His commandments, etched in stone with a blaze of glory, built the foundation for all that is moral and noble in the world. However, since their presentation, humanity has persisted in breaking God's rules, heaping trouble upon itself.

The Bible reminds us, "Love the LORD your God and keep . . . his commands always" (Deuteronomy 11:1). We don't readily grasp that God's rules are for our good. Instead of destroying individuality and enjoyment, His immutable laws protect us from harm, lead us into spiritual abundance, and grant us peace. For when we obey, we receive His blessing.

A Prayer for Blessing

Lord, I want to follow Your commands, not out of fear or coercion, but from a heart overflowing with trust for You. How can I refuse to please a lover such as You? When I obey, bless me with Your abundance. Amen.

TRIED-AND-TRUE PERENNIALS

Perennials are the return visitors to a garden. With proper care and dividing, they bloom each year, but only for a few weeks. Consequently, the key to a perennial garden is planning for a succession of blooms.

Use this chart to plan for spring, summer, and fall flowers in a perennial bed.[7] Flowering times and sizes may vary from region to region.

SPRING		
Bergenia	12 to 18 inches	Full sun to light shade
Brunnera	1 to 2 feet	Full sun to light shade
Candytuft	6 to 12 inches	Full sun
False Solomon's Seal	2 to 3 feet	Partial to full shade
Leopard's Bane	1 1/2 to 2 feet	Full sun to partial shade
Lungwort	8 to 12 inches	Full sun to partial shade
Primrose	2 to 24 inches	Partial shade
Rock Cress	6 to 12 inches	Full sun
Sandwort	2 to 8 inches	Full sun to partial shade
Solomon's Seal	2 to 3 feet	Partial to full shade
Violet (spring and fall)	3 to 12 inches	Partial shade
Wild Indigo	3 to 6 feet	Full sun

SPRING / SUMMER		
Alumroot	12 to 24 inches	Partial shade to full sun
Basket-of-Gold	6 to 12 inches	Full sun
Bleeding Heart	1 to 3 feet	Partial shade
Bluestar	1 to 3 feet	Full sun to light shade
Bugleweed	To 12 inches	Full sun to light shade
Buttercup	12 to 30 inches	Full sun to light shade
Columbine	1 1/2 to 3 feet	Full sun to light shade
Coreopsis, Tickseed	6 inches to 3 feet	Full sun
Cranesbill, Hardy Geranium	4 inches to 4 feet	Full sun to partial shade

Dead Nettle	8 to 12 inches	Partial to full shade
Flowering Onion	18 inches to 5 feet	Full sun to partial shade
Flax	12 to 24 inches	Full sun to light shade
Foxglove	2 to 5 feet	Partial shade
Gas Plant	2 to 3 feet	Full sun to light shade
Globeflower	18 inches to 3 feet	Full sun to partial shade
Lady's Mantle	12 to 18 inches	Full sun to light shade
Meadow Rue	1 to 7 feet	Full sun to partial shade
Meadowsweet	1 to 7 feet	Partial shade
Peony	18 to 36 inches	Full sun to light shade
Pink, Carnation	3 inches to 2 feet	Full sun to partial shade
Poppy	12 inches to 4 feet	Full sun to partial shade
Soapwort	6 inches to 3 feet	Full sun
Speedwell	12 to 24 inches	Full sun to partial shade
Thrift, Sea Pink	6 inches to 2 feet	Full sun

S P R I N G / S U M M E R / F A L L

Campion, Catchfly	4 inches to 2 feet	Full sun to light shade
Chrysanthemum	1 to 3 feet	Full sun to partial shade
Phlox (spring, summer, or fall)	3 inches to 4 feet	Full sun to full shade
Iris	6 inches to 5 feet	Full sun to light shade
Sage, Salvia	1 to 6 feet	Full sun
Stonecrop, Sedum	3 inches to 2 feet	Full sun to light shade
Torch Lily	2 to 4 feet	Full sun
Windflower	3 inches to 2 feet	Partial shade to full sun

S U M M E R

African Lily	3 to 5 feet	Full sun
Astilbe, False Spirea	8 inches to 3 1/2 feet	Light shade
Baby's-Breath	3 to 4 feet	Full sun
Balloon Flower	10 to 36 inches	Full sun to partial shade
Bee Balm	2 to 4 feet	Full sun to light shade
California Tree Poppy	4 to 8 feet	Full sun
Cardinal Flower, Lobelia	2 to 4 feet	Light shade
Clematis	1 1/2 to 5 feet	Full sun
Delphinium	2 to 6 feet	Full sun
Fountain Grass	2 to 5 feet	Full sun

Globe Thistle	3 to 4 feet	Full sun
Lamb's Ears, Betony	6 to 18 inches	Full sun to light shade
Lavender	1 to 3 feet	Full sun
Lupine	3 to 4 feet	Full sun to partial shade
Pincushion Flower	18 to 24 inches	Full sun
Plantain Lily, Hosta	8 inches to 3 feet	Partial to dense shade
Plume Poppy	6 to 8 feet	Full sun to partial shade
Purple Coneflower	2 to 4 feet	Full sun to light shade
Red Valerian	1 to 3 feet	Full sun
Rose Mallow, Hibiscus	3 to 8 feet	Full sun to light shade
Russian Sage	3 to 4 feet	Full sun
Sea Holly	1 to 3 feet	Full sun
Sea Lavender	18 to 30 inches	Full sun
Sundrop	6 to 24 inches	Full sun
Yarrow	6 inches to 4 1/2 feet	Full sun

SUMMER / FALL

Aster	6 inches to 8 feet	Full sun
Bellflower	6 inches to 5 feet	Full sun to light shade
Blanket-Flower	1 to 3 feet	Full sun
Boltonia	3 to 6 feet	Full sun
Bonset (until frost)	1 to 10 feet	Full sun to partial shade
Chamomile	2 to 3 feet	Full sun
Coneflower	18 inches to 6 feet	Full sun to light shade
Daylily	1 to 4 feet	Full sun to partial shade
False Dragonhead	2 to 4 feet	Full sun to partial shade
False Sunflower	3 to 5 feet	Full sun
Goldenrod	1 to 6 feet	Full sun to light shade
Hardy Begonia (until frost)	2 feet	Full sun to partial shade
Mallow	1 to 4 feet	Full sun to partial shade
Milkweed	2 to 4 feet	Full sun
Monkshood	2 to 5 feet	Light shade to full sun
Pearly Everlasting	1 to 3 feet	Full sun to light shade
Plumbago, Leadwort	8 to 12 inches	Full sun to partial shade
Sneezeweed (until frost)	2 1/2 to 6 feet	Full sun
Sunflower	3 to 7 feet	Full sun
Verbena	4 inches to 5 feet	Full sun

CHAPTER SIXTEEN

Bulbs in Barren Land

You . . . will revive me again; from the depths
of the earth you will bring me up again.

—PSALM 71:20, NRSV

There's something about cats and tulip beds.

In the short story "The Occasional Garden" the writer Saki complained, "The Darwin tulips haven't survived the fact that most of the cats in the neighborhood hold a parliament in the center of the tulip bed; that rather forlorn-looking strip that we intended to be a border of alternating geranium and spiraea has been utilized by the cat-parliament as a division lobby."[8]

I wonder if my cat Mercedes, who showed up at my front door as a stray several years ago, attended Saki's animal parliament in a past life. When we moved to this old house, a strip bulb bed already bordered the lawn's south side. Almost immediately Mercedes, by instinct or experience, plopped down in the bed and refused to budge, as if waiting to hold court.

As the seasons passed, it didn't matter what pushed up from that bed—tulips and daffodils, later dahlias and geraniums—I found Mercedes sitting in roughly the same spot, smashing whatever grew there. This flower-destroying behavior puzzled me because in other garden beds she courteously chose her steps, rarely hurting the smallest of blooms, even when stalking visitors to the neighbor's bird feeder.

Pulling Mercedes out of the bed didn't help; she returned when I retreated indoors. Sometimes neighborhood cats dropped by, but mostly Mercedes sat in the bed by herself, waiting for who-knows-what. Even when the bulb bed lay dormant.

The blooms remind me that flowers will frame the yard soon—and if I just wait, barrenness can burst into beauty.

Mercedes died last year and I miss her terribly, but I smile over the many lessons she taught me. One lesson was that much like the bulb beds, every life passes through a season of dormancy, when little or nothing seems productive. We don't have anything to show for our efforts, and though we feel like giving up, it's crucial to hang on to hope. Perhaps Mercedes sat in the bulb bed because she knew that, unlike her, I'm only marginally talented at weathering this process. I'm not fond of writing in obscurity, nor am I delighted with bulbs in barren land.

Consequently, my gardening focuses on growing herbs, annuals, and perennials, not from seeds, but from large plantings. I attribute this preference to Colorado's short growing season, but really, I find it more exciting to create an instant garden than to stare at the ground, wondering if anything beneath it is capable of movement. This means I procrastinate on planting the bulb bed, visiting nurseries after the tulip and daffodil inventories dwindle and pushing the wintry limits on planting them. One year I missed planting my bulbs altogether, and during the cold months they disintegrated into dust.

Yet despite my neglect and impatience, each spring the bulbs bloom spectacularly on cue. People walk or drive by slowly to admire the flowers. The bed fills with red, yellow, and green, and my heart swells with hope for warmer weather. Once again the blooms remind me that flowers will frame the yard soon—and if I just wait, barrenness can burst into beauty.

I'll try to remember this principle in the fall when the bulb-planting season begins, especially because I need to replace and divide them. This digging and scaling process requires more commitment than mere planting, but it ensures a hardy, enduring growth. I especially want to reform and work diligently so in the springtime I can imagine a fat cat staring at me from among the blooms, as if to say, "I told you so. You just need to believe."

Yes, there's something about cats and tulip beds.

Spiritually, we experience barren times when it seems God has failed us. We struggle with doubt, discouragement, broken dreams, unanswered prayer. We crave an expedient intervention from God, but His schedule doesn't match ours. It feels as though we've been stranded in the dirt.

During these seasons we can cling to God's promise to cultivate and spill water on our dry ground, turning despair into hope, dust into glory. If we wait on Him during the dormancy, in His time God will grant us "a garland instead of ashes, the oil of gladness instead of mourning, the mantle of praise instead of a faint spirit" (Isaiah 61:3, NRSV).

When we hope in God, His spectacular handiwork exceeds our expectations. So put your faith and hope in God (1 Peter 1:21). He is our hope, and He does not disappoint.

A Prayer for Dormant Times

Lord, teach me to wait on You during this dormancy in my life. As I feast on Your Word, remind me of Your promises to restore and invigorate me with Yourself. Fill me with the reliable hope that one day I'll walk in Your blessings. As I wait, dig me deeper into Your Word. Amen.

Although most people think of tulips and daffodils when they consider growing bulbs, there are four basic types: corms (crocus, freesia); rhizomes (iris, canna); true bulbs (tulips, hyacinths); tubers (begonia, dahlia). And though we often think of bulbs as flowers, there are also bulbous vegetables (carrots, garlic, onions, potatoes).

Each bulb type differs in its planting time, growth cycle, propagation, and preparation for winter. Yet all bulbs share one characteristic: food storage systems that promote survival and distinguish them from other plants. Remember these general points when planting bulbs.

▪ CULTIVATE DRAINED SOIL. Rot sets in if bulbs turn soggy, especially during dormancy. Clay soil soddens them, yet sandy soil drains water too fast. The ideal soil is loam, a crumbly combination of clay, sand, silt, and organic matter.

▪ WORK ON TIME. Bulbs purchased in packages include timing and planting instructions. Gardening books or local nursery owners also provide this information.

Generally, plant spring-blooming bulbs and early summer-blooming bulbs in the fall. Plant late summer-blooming bulbs from late spring to early summer; fall-blooming bulbs in the summer. Remember that bulbs sitting above ground too many months will deteriorate into dust.

▪ DIG DEEP ENOUGH. Again, pay attention to the instructions. Usually the recommended depth varies from one to eight inches. A rule of thumb is to dig a hole three times as deep as the bulb is high. Nibbly animals confiscate bulbs planted close to the earth's surface.

▪ FERTILIZE FOR GROWTH. Dig a few inches below where the bulb will sit. Work in a slow-release fertilizer or organic matter, then add back untreated dirt. Don't allow the fertilizer to rest on the bulb.

To ward off bugs, a bulb pesticide can also be worked into the soil. Shops that sell bulbs usually offer specialized fertilizers and pesticides.

▪ COVER THE BULBS with soil, tamp it down, and water.

▪ MULCH THE BED with shredded pine bark or leaves.

The Everyday Gardener

Maintaining and admiring growth

Blow on my garden, that its fragrance may spread abroad.

—Song of Songs 4:16

CHAPTER SEVENTEEN

Let There Be Light

*God saw that the light was good, and he
separated the light from the darkness.*

— GENESIS 1:4

When God proclaimed, "Let there be light," He was thinking about His garden.

Without a good source of light for extended periods of time, flowers and vegetation can't grow and bloom. For that matter, neither can any living thing, including humans. So when God commanded the sun to appear, He set in motion scientific laws that link us irrevocably to its illumination.

In my eighth-grade science class the sun's properties weren't high on my list of interests. Now I'm intrigued by its power over nature, not only affecting growth, but specifically when seeds crack open, flowers bloom, vegetables ripen, and trees and shrubs form leaves. More precisely, the garden is directly affected by the earth's latitude in relationship to the sun, the length of daylight in a particular region, and how the sun pilots seasons. While reading a book about "the unexpected science of plants, soil, sun, and seasons,"[1] I was amazed at the significance of this combination of light, length, and location. I'd simply known that plants need sunlight and often fussed over too many cloudy summer days.

Actually, to grow a garden we really only need to understand this basic light-shedding principle, but knowing slightly more extends our patience with the earth's processes. For instance, no matter how hard I try to speed them up, certain perennials stubbornly bloom at the same time each year. Why? Here is my unscientific explanation.

■ *Location and latitude.* A location's latitude (distance from the equator) affects the day length, or amount of time the sun shines, during various times of year. Day length affects plant growth and explains why certain flowers are difficult to grow in particular regions.

The upshot of this sunny business is that it's impossible to disperse a universal set of gardening tasks according to specific dates on the calendar.

"Everybody admires the gorgeous summer flower borders the British can produce, but their exuberance of phloxes, delphiniums, roses, lilies, and such has a lot to do with the fact that Britain is at a higher latitude," explains my science-and-gardening book. "British gardens get several more hours of sunshine in the summertime than most American gardens, which is why American gardens can rarely reproduce similar flower borders. It is no coincidence that the U.S. region where English-style flower borders do flourish is the Northwest; Portland and Seattle sit above the latitude of 45° north, as do London and Giverny."[2]

This alone tempts me to move to the Northwest.

■ *Cycles and seasons.* Based on their genetic disposition, plants wait for the optimum time to sprout into their growing cycles. Their genes ignite according to the amount of sunlight and types of weather, which determine periods of heat or cold, dryness and wetness. These factors explain why some regions of the country can have an earlier planting season than others, or why gardeners in a particular area harvest their crops at the same time.

Consequently, before planting it's helpful to understand a location's climate zone.

The upshot of this sunny business is that it's impossible to disperse a universal set of gardening tasks according to specific dates on the calendar. Gardeners need to understand their own locale, and this knowledge accumulates in books about specific regions and in the minds of experienced local horticulturists. Living in Colorado, I don't need garden planting advice from my aunt in Iowa or a friend in California. I'm better off talking to the neighbor next door.

Besides, the local colloquialisms about gardening can be entertaining. Native Americans told the early settlers it is time to sow seeds "when the ground is warm enough to sit upon naked and comfortable." I'm certain I'll never apply this dictum, but hearing it, I'm fascinated with the garden's pragmatic wonder.

For most of us it's easy to observe the "sunlight" in other people's lives, compared to the clouds in ours. But at best, making envious comparisons is a prescription for gloom. It hinders us from taking action, choosing productive paths, and altering what truly can be changed. Most poignantly, it obscures God's grace in our own lives. For even in the dimmest of days, we can spot His bursts of light, if we're willing to look for them.

"Give thanks in all circumstances, for this is God's will for you," says 1 Thessalonians 5:18. Thankfulness opens our eyes to God's goodness and draws us closer to Him and His life-changing miracles.

Lord, thank You for the sun and its earth-changing power—for its ability to guide the seasons, grow living things, and brighten gardens. Thanks, too, for the light of Your presence in my life, even when the days feel cold and cloudy. I will look for Your goodness in unexpected places, for I believe You give light to all Your children. Amen.

Gardeners with less-than-sunny land or gardens need not despair. There are plants that grow well in the shade. Some of the common shade plants are listed below.

Begonia

Bleeding Heart

Bugleweed

Columbine

Daylily

Elephant's Ear

Foxglove

Hosta

Ivy

Jack-in-the-Pulpit

Lily-of-the-Valley

Lobelia

Maidenhair Fern

Monkshood

Perennial Spirea

Phlox

Primrose

Snowdrop

The definition of a shade garden divides into three categories, classified by the sun's duration and intensity.

Partial shade is the sunniest classification, receiving up to six hours of sun (with at least four hours in the morning), but living in the shadows the rest of a day.

Filtered or dappled shade occurs when trees or structures such as latticework filter the sun's light, shifting its patterns and diminishing intensity.

Full shade means direct sunlight never reaches a location, though there may sometimes be reflected light.

To determine the type of shade in a garden, track the sun's patterns in the area for several days in both the winter and summer.

When purchasing foliage and flowers for a shade garden, carefully read the instructions accompanying the plants. Shade plants are designed to compete for light, and generally their leaves are large, dark, and flat. Their surfaces readily shed rainwater, protecting them from disease. Often they conserve energy by producing fewer fruits and flowers, but they are still attractive additions to a garden with limited amounts of direct sunlight.[3]

CHAPTER EIGHTEEN

Water, Water Everywhere

> *There is the sound of a heavy rain.*
> —1 KINGS 18:41

I'm about to call this The Year of the Great Rains. Not "great" in the "wonderful" sense, but in the "too much, too often" sense that washes people indoors and soggily erodes the garden. The kind that batters blooms and loosens leaves, invites insects and rots roots. The type that trickles unannounced into the basement and rusts gardening tools stored there.

This year I absolutely have not appreciated the rains. They have wielded too much power over me, withholding their refreshment when the garden needs it and later pounding the earth in furious bursts. They've confused me about when and how much to water, breaking all the rules and mocking my measly watering efforts in the face of their mighty moistening talents.

When will it rain? Right after I've finally thoroughly watered the yard myself, dragging around snakelike yards of green rubber hose. When will it quit raining? Only when the flowers and I beg for mercy. For a person who usually adores a showery afternoon, it has not been the best of summers, watching the many waters dilute my creative handiwork.

Enough rain is a blessing; too much rain is a bane. Both are a gardener's reality.

All summers are not like this, though, with water, water everywhere. Usually I welcome the rains' intermittent appearances as a party for the flowers, who perk up and dance in the afterglow. "I love the rain in the summertime," writes a gardener acquaintance from another state. "The garden looks refreshed and beautiful."

Nature seems to sense the approaching showers, whether or not we want them, whether or not we spot clouds or hear thunder.

She describes the gentle and nourishing rains, and I love what bursts forth from them too. There are the flowers, of course, but also my red rubber gardening shoes. Yellow rain slickers. Twirling umbrellas. Singing chimes hanging from downspouts. Flooded bird baths. Cooled-down air. Children splashing in puddles. The nudge to brew tea and nestle with a neglected book.

Instead of feeling frustration, I usually am lulled by the artistry and anticipation, fun and folklore, of the rains. Especially the folklore. When will it rain? *The Old Farmer's Almanac,* less cynical than I this year, tells me to watch for these signs.

- Aspen trees turn up their leaves
- Bees head for the hive
- Bread and cheese soften
- Cows become restless
- Dishes sweat
- Dogs burrow into the dirt
- Fish swim near the surface
- Flies bite

- Mushrooms sprout
- Parrots whistle
- Pitcher plants open up
- Roosters crow at evening
- Ropes shorten and twist
- Salt forms cakes
- Sheep collect in a flock
- Spiders reinforce their webs

- Flowers give off a stronger scent
- Fowl roll in the dust or sand
- Horses sweat in the stable
- Milkweed closes up
- Stars sparkle more brightly than usual
- Swallows circle and call
- Tobacco becomes moist
- Trout jump[4]

Clad in my rubber shoes, I am not the only one who anticipates the rains. Nature seems to sense the approaching showers, whether or not we want them, whether or not we spot clouds or hear thunder. We need their watering.

Even in a perplexing summer like this one, when I've grumbled at the rains' intensity, I understand that no water means no life. And in the garden, as in all things, I still want to hopefully anticipate.

I long for life.

God wants to send His rains into our spiritual lives. Not torrents that pound and destroy, but showers that bless and refresh, leaving behind growth and strength. We need not fear or feel frustrated over these rains, for they arrive at the right time and in the right measure. But we can anticipate them.

"Break up your fallow ground; for it is time to seek the LORD," instructed Hosea, "until He comes to rain righteousness on you" (Hosea 10:12, NASB). We prepare for God's showers of blessings by confessing our sin. We soak in the rains by opening our hearts to His righteousness.

A Prayer for a Well-Watered Garden

Lord, as the prophet Isaiah promised, make me "a well-watered garden, like a spring whose waters never fail." As I watch the rains fall, or when I water the garden myself, prepare my fallow heart for Your rains of righteousness. Amen.

There is no definitive rule about watering a garden, but about an inch of rain or water a week is usually enough. However, plants have differing water needs, gardens grow in many types of soil, and the weather varies from one region to another. Consequently, the following advice needs to be adjusted to a particular garden's needs.

■ WATER EARLY. Water flowers in the early morning so the moisture doesn't turn into mildew. Avoid windy or hot times when the water evaporates without reaching the plants.

■ SOAK PLANTS DEEPLY. Plants need deep waterings, not sprinklings. So instead of watering frequently but shallowly, water less frequently but deeply. Drench the soil to a depth of six inches or more.

■ WATCH FOR WILTING. When flowers wilt in the morning or evening, they're stressed and need moisture. Water them immediately. If they're wilted in the midday sun, wait to see if they bounce back in the evening. If not, water them.

A well-watered garden can flourish from various watering methods, depending on need, cost, and preference.

■ SPRINKLER. A hand-held spray attachment for a hose or a stationary sprinkler with a rotating spray will water the garden well, but use it in the morning so the moisture doesn't collect on leaves. Be sure the spray is fine; otherwise, it will destroy flowers. Don't use a full-force stream from a gardening hose to water the plants from above. It pummels the plants, shattering petals and bending stems.

■ DRIP IRRIGATION. This is the most efficient way to water because it trickles moisture directly into the plants' roots, conserving water and avoiding a buildup that invites pests and diseases. Drip irrigation can be as simple as a soaker hose (a hose with tiny holes in it) or as complicated as a commercial setup.

■ FLOOD IRRIGATION. Sometimes a stream of water at the base of a plant works best, particularly for bushes, trees, and woody vegetation. Simply hold or lay a hose at the base of the plant, allowing water to spill out and soak into the ground.

CHAPTER NINETEEN

A Stage for Growth

When it grows, it is the largest of garden plants.
—MATTHEW 13:32

The flowers come forth like the belles of the day, have their short reign of beauty and splendor, and retire, like them, to [the] more interesting office of reproducing their like. The Hyacinths and Tulips are off the stage, the Irises are giving place to the Belladonnas, as those will to the Tuberoses; as your mama has done to you, my dear Anne, as you will do to the sisters of little John, and as I shall soon and cheerfully do to you all in wishing you a long, long, good night.

—THOMAS JEFFERSON TO HIS GRANDDAUGHTER, ANNE, 1811

According to Thomas Jefferson, all the world's a stage, especially in the flower garden. Politicians knew him as the third president of the United States, but intimates and visitors to Monticello, his sweeping five-thousand-acre plantation in Virginia, understood that above all, he was a lover of the land.

Though Jefferson grew fruit, grain, grapes, vegetables, and tobacco, his gardens served as a theater in which he interacted with family members and participated in the unfolding drama of a natural world. Through the years Monticello's grounds bore flowers, but the formal gardens didn't take shape until Jefferson anticipated his retirement from the presidency. In 1807 he sketched the plans for twenty oval-shaped beds at the four corners of the house, each planted with a different kind of flower. But for Jefferson, this wasn't enough. Later he sent his granddaughter, Anne, a sketch for expansion.

Most of us won't plant and tend gardens as extensively as Jefferson did, but we still "set the stage" for our flowers to perform.

"I find that the limited number of our flower beds will too much restrain the variety of flowers in which we might wish to indulge, and therefore I have resumed an idea . . . of a winding walk . . . with a narrow border of flowers on each side. This would give us abundant room for great variety," wrote Jefferson. The winding walkways emulated the latest informal landscape design of British gardens, which he'd admired while visiting that country.[5]

Most of us won't plant and tend gardens as extensively as Jefferson did, but we still "set the stage" for our flowers to perform. We begin with enriching the soil and carefully planting our flowering hopefuls, then provide enough light and water for their growth— their "movement" across the garden's platform. Some gardeners stop working at this juncture, content to reap unpredictable reviews, but experienced earth tenders know that a successful production needs an attentive director.

We direct a garden's growth by observing its performance and coaching it toward greater drama. Practically, this requires "working hands" that touch the flower beds all season long, pulling up weeds, pouring out fertilizer, pinching off dead blooms, pruning back leaves and branches, plucking off pests, and planting new flowers in empty spaces left by predators, perennials, or reluctant performers. There are gardeners who hover over their flowers each day; there are gardeners who pull, pinch, and pluck far less. There are no etched-in-rock rules; we each find our own style and intensity of interaction. But one principle applies: Prudently but not obsessively tending the garden, rather than allowing it to grow in isolation, increases its propensity toward flourishing beauty.

As with any relationship, in the garden it's possible to be overly attentive, killing its spontaneous growth. Between too much and too little care, we need to uncover a workable balance. Striking this balance encouraged Jefferson's flowers to "come forth like the belles of the day," displaying their delicate beauty for appreciative eyes.

It's a pattern to follow, whether our flowers perform to the applause of many, or for our eyes only.

"But grow in the grace and knowledge of our Lord" (2 Peter 3:18).

When we choose a relationship with God, we "set the stage" for knowing Him better and growing in spiritual maturity. Unlike the garden, if we don't tend our spiritual selves, nothing will grow on its own. In fact, our inner life will regress and eventually die.

Conversely, if we walk in God's abundant garden, tending to what needs pinching, pruning, and pulling from our weedy lives, we can grow dramatically. Not for the admiration of others, but for His eyes only.

A Prayer for Growth

Lord, bless my flowers with Your gift of growth. But even more, visit me with Your presence. Just as I tend the garden's progress, teach me how to cultivate my relationship with You. Above all, I want to grow in the beautiful grace and knowledge of You. Amen.

There's a great debate about whether fertilizing or "feeding" a garden during its growing season is necessary.

There are gardeners who say if the soil's prepared well—tested and tilled with the appropriate amendments—it doesn't need further fertilizing. Additional nutrient-boosting elements, either organic or chemical, would be overkill and death to already nourished plants. "Like feeding beefsteak and brandy to a new-born baby," explained one professional gardener.

Other gardeners stand staunchly behind their in-season fertilizers, which contain balanced mixes of nutrients and trace minerals that boost a flower bed's growth. Fertilizers generally fall into two categories: 1) bagged, bulk fertilizers to be applied directly or sometimes diluted and 2) water-soluble fertilizers or emulsions. As discussed earlier in this book (page 46), fertilizers are marked with three numbers (0-10-10, 5-10-5, etc.) that indicate their N-P-K (nitrogen, phosphorus, potassium) components respectively. These nutrients must match the needs of specific soil types and plants in the garden.

Whatever side one chooses in the feeding debate, there's general agreement about weeding the garden. The sooner one weeds, the better. Weeds grow first in the springtime and die last in the fall. It's possible to control the weed population with mulch, which covers unwanted plant life and inhibits growth. Still, no garden is ever entirely free from weeds.

For weeding the garden, follow this expert advice: "Perennial weeds are a worse problem than annual ones. Their more extensive root systems are harder to dig out, and any fragments left behind may produce new growth. Use a digging fork with perennial weeds that have wide-spreading runners; a narrow-bladed dandelion digger is the best choice for weeds with deep roots. An onion hoe works well for cutting larger shallow-rooted annual weeds."[6]

For weeds in hard-to-reach spots, pulling them out by hand works best. Be sure to pull out the weeds' roots when the ground is slightly moist.

CHAPTER TWENTY

Seize the Day

Now is the accepted time . . . now is the day.
—2 CORINTHIANS 6:2, KJV

If I could see another Spring,
  I'd not plant summer flowers and wait:
I'd have my crocuses at once,
My leafless pink mezereons,
  My chill-veined snowdrops, choicer yet
  My white or azure violet,
Leaf-nested primrose; anything
  To blow at once, not late.

If I might see another Spring,
  I'd listen to the daylight birds
That build their nests and pair and sing,
Nor wait for mateless nightingale;

I'd listen to the lusty herds,
  The ewes with lambs as white as snow,
I'd find out music in the hail
  And all the winds that blow.

If I might see another Spring—
  Oh stinging comment on my past
That all my past results in "if"—
  If I might see another Spring
I'd laugh to-day, to-day is brief;
I would not wait for anything:
  I'd use to-day that cannot last,
  Be glad to-day and sing.[7]

—"ANOTHER SPRING"
CHRISTINA ROSSETTI, 1820-1894

If "Another Spring," is a true indication, Christina Rossetti harbored her share of regrets. If we interpret her verse literally, in the winter the poet regretted not spending more time in the recently past garden. Metaphorically speaking, she looked back and mourned not enjoying life as much as she could have. Either way we interpret her poem, most of us can identify with Christina's sentiments to some degree.

Though the gardening life serves us many joys, at some point in the growing season I think it's common to sigh about the work we "should" be doing or look back on what we could have done. This year we were going to dig up a herb bed, fix the edging around the perennials, start a backyard compost pile, paint the aging pots in the basement, win the battle against slugs once and for all. Where did the time go? Why didn't we get much done?

Gardening aspirations linger as long as we live, so if we're going to mourn anything, I suspect that most of us should regret not relaxing more.

If it's not the lost work we regret, then we complain about not having reveled in the garden. Or at least not enough. We meant to plan an outdoor party, invite friends to a patio dinner, haul out the old croquet set, recline in a lawn chair and read magazines, stroll through the garden in the mornings. Why didn't we?

I've had these regrets and questions myself, but I'm learning to chalk them up as time wasters. In one sense, we need a seize-the-day mentality in the garden. If aphids have landed on the petunias, if sneaky vines are choking the climbing roses, we need to rescue our plants quickly. In the middle of a dry spell, we should water more frequently. If the soil is leached of nutrients, we need to replenish it. If we don't pay attention to some tasks, we're sure to reap cause-and-effect regrets. But I think most of our "if only" complaints stem not so much from the earth's demands as from a pressing desire to constantly expand the gardening horizon, or to create an unobtainable perfection.

Gardener Henry Mitchell exemplifies this tendency. "If the colors don't seem right . . . move the plants around until you like them better. When you shift things about, you get a good many surprises, and commonly one partner of an especially satisfying color group will promptly die. No matter. We just keep at it, and presumably we will get it all worked out the year after we die."[8]

Gardening aspirations linger as long as we live, so if we're going to mourn anything, I suspect that most of us should regret not relaxing more. Or regret the wasted time spent on regrets. It is not the garden blaming us that we didn't work hard enough; it is ourselves.

The garden knows there is always next year.

When we're emotionally mired in regret, the Lord tells us, "Forget the former things; do not dwell on the past. See, I am doing a new thing! Now it springs up; do you not perceive it? I am making a way in the desert and streams in the wasteland" (Isaiah 43:18-19).

God asks that we look around at what He's doing now, look ahead to a redemptive future, and look up to Him as our guide. When we focus on following Him, there is no need to look back. He only asks that we seize this day.

A Forward-Looking Prayer

Lord, I surrender my gardening regrets and the "should have" circumstances of my life to You. Pull me away from the past and point me in a new direction. Create in me a forward-thinking attitude, looking ahead to memorable times with You. Amen.

No matter what we do, insects and other pests will always visit our gardens. They thrive on the soil, water, and plants there, and in one sense they are a fact of gardening life. On the other hand, there are ways to create a more pest-resistant garden.

Though the gardener needs to learn particular methods for specific bugs and crawlers, some methods include:

■ HEALTHY SOIL. If the soil has been amended and supplied with the appropriate nutrients, plants will grow vigorous, maximizing their ability to withstand pests.

■ PEST-RESISTANT PLANTS. Planting pest-immune and pest-resistant plants helps keep the bugs at bay. Horticulturists classify plants according to their ability to repel pests. Plants marked "immune" indicate they can't be harmed by certain pests. Those called "resistant" rarely are infested by specific predators and suffer little damage if they are attacked. "Tolerant" describes plants that are subject to infestation but can survive without permanent damage. "Susceptible" plants are highly vulnerable to one or more pests. Avoid these.

■ NATIVE PLANTS. Many native plants are already resistant to native pests. A local Cooperative Extension Service can identify natives plants for a specific area.

■ PROPER MAINTENANCE. The appropriate amounts of water, fertilizer, and clean-up in the garden assist the pest-riddance process. For example, too much water attracts slugs, and dead leaves and spent flowers can hide a variety of pests.

■ PRUNING DISEASE. If a stem or branch looks infested, cutting it away from the plant inhibits the spread of destruction.

■ BARRIERS AND TRAPS. Nurseries and garden shops sell a variety of traps, barriers, and protective covers for catching and/or destroying pests, both large and small.

■ ORGANIC INSECTICIDES. Made from natural materials, organic insecticides can destroy pests without harming the environment.[9]

CHAPTER TWENTY-ONE

The Language of Flowers

*Flowers appear on the earth; the season
of singing has come.*

—SONG OF SONGS 2:12

Tiger-lily!" said Alice, addressing herself to one that was waving gracefully about in the wind,
"I wish you could talk!"

"We can talk," said the Tiger-lily, "when there's anybody worth talking to."

Alice was so astonished that she couldn't speak for a minute: it seemed quite to take her
breath away. At length, as the Tiger-lily only went on waving about, she spoke again, in a timid
voice—almost in a whisper. "And can all the flowers talk?"

"As well as you can," said the Tiger-lily. "And a great deal louder." [10]

— *THROUGH THE LOOKING GLASS*
LEWIS CARROLL, 1832-1898

We won't hear audible voices from them, as Alice did in *Through the
Looking Glass*, but flowers do possess a language of their own. Aside
from their Latin names, which most of us don't know how to decipher, the
flowers we grow and give can connote common meanings and messages to their receivers.

A small book sitting on my living room end table, called the *Language of*

Flowers, contains handwritten lists of flowers and their meanings. It's a copy of a handmade version dedicated simply "To Mother, Wishing you many happy returns of the day, from Father. August 18, 1913." Besides perusing its charming information, I've consulted the book for sending flowers that communicate special messages to friends.

The rose, which generally means "love," takes on many meanings, depending on its specific name or species. I particularly enjoy scanning the lists for the rose's special pronouncements. According to my treasured book, these are the meanings of some roses existent at the turn of the century, when the anonymous author penned his book.

When we use the language of flowers to give gifts or grace a table setting,... they can deliver an even deeper message to our hearts.

ROSE	MEANING	ROSE	MEANING
Austrian	Thou art all that is lovely	John Hopper	Encouragement
Bridal	Happy love	Maiden Blush	If you love me, you will find out
Burgundy	Unconscious beauty		
Cabbage	Ambassador of love	Musk	Capricious beauty
Campion	Only deserve my love	Red Rosebud	Pure and lovely
Carolina	Love is dangerous	Single Rose	Simplicity
China	Beauty always new	Thornless	Early attachment
Christmas	Relieve my anxiety	White	I am worthy of you
Damask	Brilliant complexion	White & Red	Unity
Deep Red	Bashful shame	Yellow	Decrease of love, jealousy [11]

Not many people know these meanings, so I'm not upset if I receive yellow roses, but a note about a flower's meaning, attached to a bouquet, can speak volumes. When a friend grieved a loss, I sent Lily-of-the-Valley flowers and a card that noted, *Lily-of-the-Valley means "return of happiness."* They represented our hope for her future and reminded us that wounds eventually heal.

Still, when we use the language of flowers to give gifts or grace a table setting, whether snipped from a cutting garden or arranged by the florist, they can deliver an even deeper message to our hearts. "Blossoms are the essence of God's gift of life on earth," explains gardener Lois Trigg Chaplin. "We see that as different as each kind may be, they all proclaim the eternity, intelligence, and grace of their Creator."[12]

Flowers remind us that God has given His best to us, for He speaks the language of love.

A Prayer for Meaning

Lord, when I give flowers from the garden, I will bestow them wholeheartedly. Let them bring cheer and meaning to the receivers, deepening our relationship and reminding us of Your good gifts to us. Amen.

"Every good and perfect gift is from above, coming down from the Father of the heavenly lights, who does not change like shifting shadows," wrote the apostle James (1:17). Certainly the garden is the Creator's great gift to us, but we can remember that every good thing, every good relationship, every good circumstance is from Him. When He created the earth, God "saw that it was good" (Genesis 1:12), and He's specialized in good gifts ever since.

"Surely God is good . . . to those who are pure in heart" (Psalm 73:1), and we can depend on His goodness for a lifetime.

CUT-AND-DRY BEAUTIES

A cutting garden can help us express sentiments through the language of flowers. This garden is utilitarian in purpose, planted in dense rows, and grows blooms to be snipped and arranged for indoor enjoyment.

The following annuals[13] and perennials[14] work well for cutting gardens, whether blooms are kept in vases or hung upside down to dry. The flowers suggested for fresh arrangements have "long vase lives." Those listed for drying retain their color, making attractive flower arrangements all year long.

FRESH ARRANGEMENTS		DRIED ARRANGEMENTS	
ANNUALS	PERENNIALS	ANNUALS	PERENNIALS
Bachelor's-Button	Aster	Bells of Ireland	Astilbe
Bishop's Flower	Baby's-Breath	Celosia	Baby's-Breath
China Aster	Bellflower	Everlasting, Immortelle	Delphinium
Cosmos	Blanket-Flower	Everlasting, Strawflower	Fernleaf Yarrow
Dahlia	Chrysanthemum	Globe Amaranth	Gay-Feather
Mexican Sunflower	Coneflower	Gomphocarpus	Globe Thistle
Pot Marigold	Delphinium	Honesty	Lamb's Ear
Prairie Gentian	False Sunflower	Notchleaf Static	Lavender
Rocket Larkspur	Flowering Onion	Paper Moon	Ornamental Onion
Snapdragon	Foxglove	Prince's-Feather	Pearly Everlasting
Sweet-Sultan	Gay-Feather	Quaking Grass	Sea Lavender
	Globe Thistle		Strawflower
	Goldenrod		Sea Holly
	Iris		Sneezewort
	Lavender		White Mugwort
	Meadow Rue		Yarrow
	Peony		
	Phlox		
	Purple Coneflower		
	Sea Holly		

CHAPTER TWENTY-TWO

Friendship Feasts

Let's have a feast and celebrate.
—LUKE 15:23

When the perennials bend in full bloom or fall nips the air, my brain automatically clicks in and says, "It's time for an outdoor dinner party." I want to share the garden's rewards with the people in my life before the flowers fade.

Dining al fresco deeply appeals to me, perhaps awakening a primal desire to connect with the earth and partake of its bounty. Because my family lives miles away, I focus on sharing the garden's rewards with an assortment of friends, and planning combinations of food, flowers, and folks never fails to stir my creative instincts and spark my imagination. I can spend hours cooking a meal, creating table settings, cleaning the house, and caring for flowers beds, enjoying every moment of the anticipation. Regarding design and hospitality, I believe details evoke delight; but if I'm not careful, too many ideas can sap my energy before the guests arrive.

Last year I threw a Fourth of July party in the backyard, complete with red, white, and blue decorations and tableware, flaming torches staked in the yard, and a huge flag and twinkling lights draped on the back deck. Two days before the event I weeded, trimmed, and added new blooms to the flower beds, and on Independence Day I cooked for hours, even though I'd ordered the main dishes from a caterer. By the time friends arrived for the early dinner, I wished I could crawl into bed and let them fend for themselves.

Not a good way to hostess a party, I chided myself while playing an after-dinner game of croquet in the semilight, struggling to stay awake. *I've got to change my mode of operation*. Outdoors or inside, my dinner parties were always a success, full of lively conversation and delicious food, but I was knocking myself out in the process.

Nature provides the decoration, the unifying icebreaker for visitors, and an ongoing conversation piece.

Since then I've recalled the memorable outdoor meals I've eaten, and I've been struck by their common bond of simplicity. A picnic at the zoo. Grilling in an open-door garage when the rain wouldn't relent. Bread, cheese, and salad eaten by a goldfish pond in a compact and high-walled urban garden. A thrown-together pasta meal where I introduced two women who talked into the darkness as table candles burned into puddles. A circle of beloved friends eating takeout food on a patio, surrounded by a woodsy backyard.

Consequently, I've realized that a friendship feast in the garden needn't be a complicated affair, full of time-consuming plans and preparation. When a meal is served outside, nature provides the decoration, the unifying icebreaker for visitors, and an ongoing conversation piece. While the sun and breeze, birds and blooms do the "work" of entertaining, I can serve simple foods and concentrate on the most important component of hospitality: the guests. They are the true "feast" at hand, not the food or the ambiance.

However, this doesn't require that I never entertain with the china or silver, or prepare a thoughtful table setting for the outdoors. It's that I needn't let harried activity overtake genuine hospitality, which nurtures and replenishes the soul of everyone present—including mine.

"As a tonic for a troubled world, friendship and behaving with consideration and care may seem light and even frivolous, but that could be because we have lost a sensitivity to the values of the soul," claims Thomas Moore in his book *Soul Mates*.[15] Hospitality can revive this sensitivity and nurture the souls passing through our homes. Particularly, hospitality in the garden serves up sensory feasts we can't create, for they are the Lord's handiwork.

"A garden makes a delightful dining room. Divinely decorated, tirelessly making itself over, only a garden can surprise its guests with such marvels as the newly burst bulb or the exquisite hummingbird," explains garden entertainer Patricia Horan. "With our gardens we are creatures of the season, the mood, and the moment, and we like each other's company."[16]

Most of all, we are God's creatures, humbly sharing His presence.

ℜℰℭ

The Lord invites us to His spiritual feast.

He calls, "Come, all you who are thirsty, come to the waters; and you who have no money, come, buy and eat! Come, buy wine and milk without money and without cost. Why spend money on what is not bread, and your labor on what does not satisfy? Listen, listen to me, and eat what is good, and your soul will delight in the richest of fare. Give ear and come to me; hear me, that your soul may live" (Isaiah 55:1-3).

A Prayer for a Garden Meal

Lord, we gather today in the garden, grateful for Your presence with us. Together, we feast on Your simple abundance around us. Bless the meal we eat, and continue to multiply the fruits of this garden. Amen.

Into the Garden

GATHERING AMONG THE FLOWERS

BY PATRICIA HORAN

Your garden's best entertaining spot may very well move during the year, depending on what blooms where during each season.

An overhanging tree that shelters a small luncheon party from the sun in midsummer also prevents an early spring sun from making its debut. Even the view from an established spot will change as trees grow and lose their leaves.

Look carefully, with fresh eyes, at the views from various garden locations. Take some photographs to remind yourself of how a spot will look at a given time in the year. Hesitate before you plan a party near a rose bush that is busy with bees—and be aware that a tree that attracts bees in the spring will usually bring birds in the fall.

It is not possible to have all areas of the garden in top form for the entire year, so different spots should be focused on during different months. Veteran garden hosts and hostesses agree that the spots that will be most welcoming to your guests will almost always be those areas you naturally gravitate to with your cup of morning coffee or your afternoon iced tea on non-party days.

The grace of a well-tended garden is that it is never, no matter what season, uninviting.

Even in the snows of coldest winter, a stroll along a path, a mug of mulled cider in hand, can lift the heart.

The garden, whatever the time of year, is never closed or inaccessible to the partying viewer, whether observed from inside or out. There is no "off season." The garden never has a "down time" but can always be relied upon to enhance or enchant a gathering. The garden is always busy changing, working with nature to show us its wonders, speaking to us as long as we take the time to listen and learn its ways.[17]

Try these ideas to enhance your party giving in the garden. Most of these suggestions use flowers or garden-related items to exercise your creativity and delight visitors.

Party Favors

These inexpensive party favors can be given to visitors as they arrive, positioned near each place setting, served with dessert, or handed to guests as they leave.

- Arrange flowers in small dispenser cups

- Create single-flower corsages from the garden

- Fill tiny terra-cotta pots with nuts or candy

- Give inexpensive gardening tools or supplies

- Hand out seed packets or bags of bulbs

- Make rosewater from rose petals; pour into miniature bottles

- Plan a gardening treasure hunt, allowing guests to take home their "finds"

- Pull blooms from the main flower arrangement for take-home gifts

- Press dried flowers onto handwritten welcome notes

- Write out gardening poems on flowered stationery, to be read at the meal

Table Decorations

Choose a few of these ideas for decorating the serving and dining tables.

- Arrange gardening utensils in plant pots

- Create placecards with flowers pressed into them

- Design several small flower arrangements for each table

- Garnish each plate with herbs or flower heads

- Hang flower swags on the back of each chair

- Make candles with flowers poised in the hardened wax

- Pin fresh flowers to the edges of the tablecloth

- Place a single rose or other flower in each folded napkin

- Place pots of forced bulbs on the table

- Put a flower in a bud vase at each place setting

- Sprinkle fresh petals, leaves, or vines across the table

- Use ice cubes with mint leaves frozen into them

- Wrap viney flowers around the glass or flatware stems

Yard Adornments

These ideas will help decorate the yard for both day and night.

- Arrange a birdhouse display

- Attach a flower swag or wreath to the gate

- Drop flower petals into a pond or birdbath

- Hang bouquets of dried flowers or herbs from tree branches

- Light the yard with flower-fragrant torches

- Line the walks with luminaria (bags with lit candles) with leaf and flower cutouts

- Place potted flowers throughout the lawn

- Position lighted candles on the deck, patio, and walkways

- String white lights in the trees or along the fence

- Wrap viny flowers around lawn furniture or table legs and chairs

AFTER-DARK PERFORMANCES

Planning an evening dinner or party outdoors doesn't mean your guests have to miss the garden's aromas and beauty. You can plant flowers that bloom after dark. Try plants with white or light-colored flowers and those with fragrance in the evening.

These flowers perform after dark.

Astilbe	Nocturnal Daylily
Bouncing Bet	Nocturnal Water Lily
Brugmansia	Oriental Lily
Confederate Jasmine	Peacock Orchid
Cosmos	Pot Marigold, White
Cup-and-Saucer Vine	Siberian Iris
Dahlia	Spider Flower
Evening Primrose	Sunflower
Evening Stock	Tree Mallow
Four O' Clocks	Turtlehead
Foxglove	White Poppy
Fragrant Plantain Lily	Yucca [18]
Gas Plant	
Gay's Delight	
Geranium, White	
Giant Hogweed	
Gourd	
Honeysuckle	
Impatiens	
Love-in-a-Mist	
Mock Orange	
Moonflower Vine	
Nicotiana	
Night Phlox	

According to gardener Peter Loewer, "The fragrance of an evening garden is different from the fragrance of a daylight garden. Day-blooming flowers usually have light, pleasant odors that, along with their bright colors, attract butterflies, hummingbirds, and daytime insects. Night-bloomers, or those with heightened nighttime fragrance, usually have a heavier scent." [19]

The Faithful Garden

PREPARING FOR THE SEASON TO COME

As long as the earth endures,
seedtime and harvest, cold and heat, summer and winter,
day and night will never cease.

—GENESIS 8:22

CHAPTER TWENTY-THREE

Putting the Earth to Bed

It was you who set all the boundaries of the
earth; you made both summer and winter.

—PSALM 74:17

For the gardener, the fall fills with suspense. When will Jack Frost arrive with his growth-stopping performance? When will nature drop its final curtain? When should we begin preparing the earth for its cold slumber? The rest of the world may unknowingly slip into winter, but gardeners cannot. We have questions to ask, tasks to do. As the weather cools we simultaneously close down one growing season and prepare for another; it is a time of both loss and expectation.

Where I live nature plays autumn tricks with gardeners, blurring the lines between seasons and stealing blooms in stages. Sometime from mid to late September a vindictive frost visits our grounds, finishing off the impatiens, begonias, and other tender flowers. Waking up to blackened and broken plants, my mind turns to winter. But just when I've cajoled myself into accepting the garden's decline, the weather shifts and disguises itself as an Indian summer. For several more weeks the garden is half-withered, half-bloomed, as the days climb up to a pleasant warmth, but the nights gradually descend toward coldness.

In my initial years of gardening, I fought the first frost and its unpredictable cousins who arrived later in October. Armed with newspapers and old bed sheets, and then light-weight garden blankets sold by a nursery supply company, I stole into the brisk darkness, covering up the flower beds to protect them from harm. It was a game of sorts. Even after monitoring the weather reports, it was impossible to tell which nights would bring frost and which would make my elaborate cover-ups laughable.

It's more important that I ensure a plant's season-to-season life than its short-term presence in the autumn yard.

I also had unanswerable questions. *If I take the blankets off this morning, will I need to reapply them tonight? Should I leave them on for a few days, in case there are successive cold nights?* If I left the coverings on in the daytime, it obscured my view of the flowers and defeated my goal of prolonging the garden's pleasures. If I took them off, I got caught in the time-consuming act of folding and unfolding the stiffened material, sometimes twice a day.

After a few years of hit-and-miss effort, I gave up. Nature always eventually won anyway, so I decided to let my flowers depart naturally. I still protect herbs so I have time to harvest them, but for the most part I now regard the first frost as a signal to ready the garden for winter. As veteran gardeners say, I need to "put the garden to bed." And there is plenty to do.

"As the long summer days grow shorter and evenings become chilly, gardeners in cold-winter climates embark on the last and most important tasks of the garden year—the ones that make the difference between whether some plants will live or die," explain the gardening experts at the Smith & Hawken company. "Just as in early autumn you make sure the car has plenty of antifreeze to protect the engine, this is the time to provide protection for your plants."[1]

So for me, fall has switched from worrying about cover-ups to winterizing the flowers beds. It's more important that I ensure a plant's season-to-season life than its short-term presence in the autumn yard.

Consequently, I've adopted this wisdom from a seasoned gardener. "By October, [there should be] nothing much left to worry about. The summer annuals are nearing their end or have already been pulled up. The autumn perennials don't mind the early frosts, and planted pots that have been summering out-of-doors should have been taken in long ago. It is a peaceful moment. Signs of decay, of imminent death, come as a relief after a fruitful season, and the sinister words 'killing frost' hold no terror for me. It will all begin again, soon enough."[2]

For the garden and the gardener, there needs to be rest.

For the wintry times in our lives, we can remember Jesus Christ's words: "Come to me, all you who are weary and burdened, and I will give you rest . . . I am gentle and humble in heart, and you will find rest for your souls" (Matthew 11:28-29).

God gives His people seasons and spaces to rest—extended periods when both physically and spiritually we cuddle down and accept the refurbishing rewards of a well-deserved slumber. These times are crucial preparation for the growing days ahead, so instead of wearying ourselves further by staving them off, we benefit from simply curling up to rest in the Father's sheltering arms.

A Prayer for the Coming Cold

Lord, while putting the earth to bed, I think of how I can rest safely in You. Keep me filled with Your warmth so the world's coldness won't harm me. Help me to prepare for and wisely pass through life's wintry days, tucked in Your comforting arms. Amen.

COLD FRAMES FOR WINTRY DAYS

BY THE EDITORS OF SMITH & HAWKEN

By controlling weather conditions, cold frames can extend a growing season or, more commonly, begin one earlier than outside conditions allow—a boon for starting seeds and hardening off. In areas with not-too-severe winters, cold frames enable gardeners to grow hardy crops (like lettuce and spinach) in the winter. When seated over flower beds, they also provide winter protection for tender perennials. In summer, topless cold frames placed in a shaded area can be used to start cold-weather seeds for fall crops.

These enclosed structures consist of a framed transparent lid that sits on top of a bottomless rectangular box whose sides slope down toward the front at a 45° angle.

Glass or Plexiglas is used for commercial lids; old sash-type windows or storm windows are traditional in homemade cold frames. If home-constructed, the banked wood base (3/4" plywood is an acceptable lumber) should be treated with linseed oil and caulk to ensure a water-tight seal. Portable cold frames come in models that collapse when not in use; larger ones obviously remain in place.

The cold frame collects solar heat, warming its interior when exposed to full sunlight. An interior painted white or lined with foil will increase reflective light, useful in the coldest climates. A site facing south prolongs sunlight exposure and is recommended.

An old blanket is useful for covering the frame during a prolonged winter freeze.

A cold frame requires monitoring to prevent plant-burning and disease. The inside temperature can get very hot. One warm day with the lid closed can steam your plants. Maintain a favorable temperature (a thermometer is essential), and provide ventilation by opening and shutting the lid. If you're short on time, look for a cold frame with an automatic vent that opens and closes, adjusting to changes in temperature. You can also buy such a mechanism to attach to a homemade cold frame.

Water early in the day, and frequently; the heat in a cold frame quickly evaporates moisture. [3]

CHAPTER TWENTY-FOUR

Winter Dreams and Doings

Here is my dream.
—DANIEL 4:9

The garden on Turkey Hill Road is in repose, frozen solid, its growth halted. But I, the gardener, am not at rest. All during the Christmas holidays the mailbox was filled to brimming every day with catalogues of all descriptions, each presaging the newest, the biggest, the best, and the most unusual in seeds, nursery stock, and summer bulbs. My mind races; whatever modest plans I had formulated after the last year's blooming season are now expanded beyond all reason.

I force myself to stop, take a deep breath, and reexamine every aspect of my overall garden plan. Then order forms are greedily filled in.... I send off the orders for the long-season annuals—the snapdragons, impatiens, and the ruffled petunias (pink, white, and magenta this time) so that I will be able to sow them in the greenhouse before it is too late. I forgo the latest movies to start the lobelias and slip the ivies for the urns, and put off dinners with friends to putter for hours, mixing potting soils, washing down the greenhouse, and attending to the topiaries.[4]

— GARDENING
MARTHA STEWART, 1991

Thus begins the chapter titled "January" in a gardening book by Martha Stewart, our generation's ubiquitous home-management guru. Hers was one of the first books I purchased when eager to learn about gardening, and I remember being surprised that it initiated a year's horticultural ventures with a section called "Winter" rather than "Spring."

Gardening tasks in the winter? According to Martha, the correct answer was yes. During January her journal received these entries:

- Reviewed garden plans
- Visited gardens to study landscaping
- Gathered catalogues
- Began seed orders

- Ordered roses and trees
- Thoroughly cleaned greenhouse
- Started herb seeds in greenhouse
- Rooted slips for edgings and urns

In contrast, if I'd kept a gardening journal at that time, my January entries would have looked like this:

- Collapsed after the Christmas rush
- Thought about reading my pile of gardening books, but never got to them
- Watched videos of movies I missed during good outdoor weather
- Almost forgot to water the geraniums I brought in for the winter
- Wished I had money to purchase seeds and supplies

Over the years I've learned that for the gardener, in addition to rest, winter is a time for wide-awake visions about things to come.

As much as I admire Martha and use her ideas, at this point she disheartened me. I felt lazy and undisciplined, whiling away the winter without purpose. I needed to consider how to use those months for planning and preparation, not to keep up with Martha, but to stop the springtime from cramming too many activities in too few days. So here is my modest list for this winter:

- Clean gardening pots and tools

- Peruse the catalogs for ideas

- Make lists of and purchase tools and supplies

- Read gardening books

- Dream about and plan next summer's garden

Spread over four months, it's a manageable amount of work, free from springtime's ticking earth clock, but full of meaningful dreams and doings. Over the years I've learned that for the gardener, in addition to rest, winter is a time for wide-awake visions about things to come. Sitting in stuffed chairs by firesides, sipping hot cocoa, perusing mail-order catalogs, and weaving fantasies about future flowers, we can still enjoy the garden. These are the lulling days of winter. A time of memories and imagination. A foretaste of the season to come.

"Where there is no vision, the people perish," warns Proverbs 29:18 (KJV), underscoring the importance of using life's barren days to hope and dream about the future. "Outside" the forecast may look bleak, but inside the soul we can stoke the embers of faith. Despite the circumstances, we can believe in better days to come.

We can believe because we serve a God who unbundles our cares, warms us with His tender words, and replenishes us for the next part of our journey. Just as winter assuredly melts into spring, God is faithful to us, lighting fires in hearts grown cold.

MORE TOOLS FOR THE TRADE

For the gardener, it seems one can never own enough tools. So here is more advice for buying and caring for those all-important implements.

THE NEVER-ENDING LIST

Even in the winter, nurseries stock gardening tools, and it's a good time to leisurely shop for new and replacement items. After buying the basics (see page 66), the gardener's tool list can expand into an array of possibilities, so this after-the-basics list could prove helpful.

▪ BULB PLANTER, either short- or long-stemmed, to dig deep and consistent holes for bulbs.

▪ BYPASS PRUNER for trimming stalks, spindly branches, and blooms such as roses. When in motion the two blades bypass each other, allowing close contact with the plant.

▪ DIBBER, made in small to large sizes, to poke holes in the ground for seeds and small bulbs.

▪ HEDGE TRIMMER to cut, trim, and prune shrubbery. Either hand or power generated.

▪ LAWN RAKE to clean up dead leaves and other debris in the yard.

▪ LOPPERS with handles longer than a hedge trimmer, to reach and prune tree limbs.

▪ MATTOCK, often called pick and hoe, with a broad blade on one end and a pick on the other, to break up hard soil and cut through roots.

▪ PITCHFORK with lightweight tines to pitch hay or aerate the compost pile. If a heavier tool is preferred, use a digging fork which looks similar but has wider tines.

▪ SHARPENING STONE for keeping tool blades in top condition.

▪ SOAKER HOSES, designed to slowly leak water into the ground, away from foliage.

▪ SPRAY SPRINKLER to water flower beds with a misty spray.

▪ WATERING CAN, available in various sizes and materials, for watering potted plants and applying liquid fertilizer.

Though it's best to care for tools immediately after using them during the growing season, wintertime also is a time to repair and spruce up gardening implements. Gardener Celia Barbour offers these tips for tool tune-ups.

▪ CLEAN RUSTY PARTS. "Solvents such as lighter fluid and Liquid Wrench are good for tough clean-up jobs. To remove rust from long-neglected tools, cut a scouring pad (such as Scotch-Brite) into manageable pieces, then dampen a piece with solvent and use it to scrub away the rust. When finished, wipe clean. Solvent also helps loosen rusted screws and ease creaky joints."

▪ REPLACE BLADES. "When nicks and dents in the blades become so severe that they can't be honed away, it's time to replace the blades. Unscrew the pivot bolt and nut assembly, remove the lock, and pop off the old blade. A gentle push helps snap the new one into place. Clean all the parts with solvent and lubricate them lightly with WD-40 before reattaching them. It's also a good idea to replace the spring between handles every year or two, to keep the tool flexible."

▪ SHARPEN DULL BLADES. Various tools need specific types of sharpening.

Hoes, Loppers, Pruners, Secateurs: "With an ordinary drill, you can put a keen edge on these tools in a few minutes. Attach [a] Multi-Sharp rotary sharpener to the drill, start it spinning, then lower it gently against the edge of the tool."

Shears: "Attach a good sharpener to a corner of your workbench, and whenever scissors or shears turn dull, quickly hone a fine edge back onto the blades."

▪ *Shovels:* "A bastard file is the traditional tool used for sharpening shovels, hoes, and edgers, and works fine—though it takes more effort than the rotary sharpener."

▪ TAPE HANDLES. "Deep cracks require a new handle to be safe, but mere splinters can be prevented from worsening with ordinary hockey-stick tape, available at sporting-goods stores. Begin several inches beyond the crack, and wrap the tape tightly around the handle, with each revolution overlapping the previous layer of tape by one-half to two-thirds the width of the tape. Repeat with a second layer of tape for heavy-weight tools."[5]

Journal Jots and Thoughts

Once the Christmas season rush subsides, it's an opportune time to review your gardening journal. If you jotted down notes during the summer, you can consult them to evaluate these aspects of the last gardening year.

- What worked well about the various flower bed designs? What did not?

- Which flowers flourished in the garden? Which did not? Why?

- What pest and disease problems do you need to solve? How can you?

- How did various fertilizers, amendments, and other gardening aids perform?

- What new gardening information and techniques do you want to learn?

- What new tools would you like for the next season? Which need repair?

- What flowers do you want to repeat next year?

- What seeds and bulbs do you need to order for the next season?

- What new annuals and perennials do you want to purchase for next season?

A gardening journal for the next growing season should suit your working needs and level of interest in entering information into a diary. You can purchase a gardening journal (also called diaries or day books) or create your own. Your new gardening journal can include space for any of these suggestions.

- Calendar for recording daily gardening activities

- Lists of things to do each month

- Lists of favorite annuals, perennials, herbs, and bulbs

- Graphs for designing flowers beds and gardens

- Lists of equipment to buy, replace, or repair

- Notations about regional nuances and weather patterns

- Lists of flower seeds to sow indoors and outdoors

- Notations about soil and its amendments

- Lists of new flowers and bulbs to acquire

- Notations about garden maintenance: mulching, lighting, watering, fertilizing

- Problems and how they are solved (weeds, bugs, diseases)

- Lists of nurseries, garden clubs, horticultural societies

- Names and addresses of flower gardening catalogs

- Clippings and pressed flowers

- Spiritual and personal thoughts about gardening

CHAPTER TWENTY-FIVE

The Snowy Garden

The tempest comes out from its chamber,
the cold from the driving winds.

—JOB 37:9

Sometimes in the depth of winter I crunch around the backyard, poking gloved fingers into the snowy flower beds, daring myself to find signs of life. Compared to my Midwestern upbringing, the winters here in Colorado, though unpredictable, seem mild and considerate of a person's need to know there's still earth underneath her feet. At times white drifts heap against the house, but within days they dissolve in the persistent sun. We're fortunate in this part of the state. Nestled at the base of the Rockies, we miss the perpetually snowed-in mountains of February.

When the snow is low and the ground visible, I conduct my winter walkabouts. I should know better by now, but I'm always surprised by what I find. Usually a few cut-back perennials still sport some green leaves, the sweet woodruff ground cover hasn't died back completely, and chives push up in the cold, defying the conventional winter wisdom of most plants. I gather hope from these diehards. If they can hang on through the frozen days, so can I. They remind me that it won't be long before the crocuses appear and bulb beds begin stirring in the sunlight.

Some day, instead of rummaging around for the unexpected, I'd like to plant an intentional winter garden—the type in which green and brown textures wave in the wind and defy the chilliest of days. Though I enjoy discovering snowy surprises, I'd appreciate the certainty of some plant activity while most of the flowers hide. It would reassure me that the garden isn't dead; it is merely asleep. Just thinking about this cheers me.

When most outdoor blooms have months ago fallen next to retiring foliage, there is no need to abandon the garden entirely.

Books in my gardening library tell me it's possible to muster a garden in winter, suggesting I invest in these hardy plants:

- Corkscrew Willow
- Creeping Juniper
- English Ivy
- Evergreen Wintercreeper
- Gray Birch
- Horsetail
- Lenten Rose

- Purple Moor Grass
- Russian Olive
- Sensitive Fern
- Siberian Cypress
- Staghorn Sumac
- Stonecrop Willow
- Yucca[6]

My winter garden probably won't materialize until I have a bigger yard, but even without these cold weather plants, I won't miss out on my snowy walks. "The cold may chill our noses and that ominous stripe of weak orange light across the horizon may presage more snow, but it will not stop us from a walk in the winter garden," insists the garden writer Peter Loewer.[7] These walks bolster my spirits, ward off cabin fever, and evoke good memories from summer.

They also spark ideas for bringing nature indoors. I like to gather up pine cones for the fireplace mantle and cut fruit tree branches for budding in a dining table vase. They join the abandoned bird nests, dried herbs and flowers, and forced bulbs already in the house, all representatives of gardens past and those to come. And of course, for a month there are the evergreen trees, wreaths, boughs, berries, and garlands of Christmas.

So take heart. When most outdoor blooms have months ago fallen next to retiring foliage, there is no need to abandon the garden entirely. According to her writings, Gertrude Jekyll perked up houses all winter long with garden discoveries. "A very few flowers can be made to look cleverly arranged with plenty of good foliage; and even when a hard and long frost spoils the few blooms that would otherwise be available, leafy branches alone are beautiful in rooms," she advised, and suggested arranging with "the exercise of good taste."[8]

I don't think it requires a staggering sense of style to place branches in a vase, though. And even if someone should question our taste, it really doesn't matter. Bringing snowy garden plants and branches indoors comforts us. In a unique way, they are the harbingers of spring.

Just when it feels like we'll collapse into a snowy heap, God grabs our hands and invites us to walk with Him in the wintertime. It is an assurance of both security and surprise.

If the path turns narrow and we can't see Him behind us, the Lord promises, "Whether you turn to the right or to the left, your ears will hear a voice behind you, saying, 'This is the way; walk in it'" (Isaiah 30:21). And in that way, we discover unexpected joys that He has buried in the cold.

A Prayer for Winter Discoveries

Lord, I share this winter walk in the garden with You. As we pass time together, show me the surprises of nature, the unexpected joys of life with You. Be my personal guide and herald of the springtime to come. Amen.

Into the Garden

A GREENHOUSE GETAWAY

BY LARRY HODGSON AND T. JEFF WILLIAMS

The world of greenhouses is a world of magic, a world in which seasons and climates don't matter. In a greenhouse, flowers bloom the year round, exotic fruits thrive, and fresh vegetables are ripe for picking in winter.

The lure of the greenhouse is powerful. When you walk inside, you shut yourself off from the frenzied world outside. You work in the soil and putter around even during cold or stormy weather. You can tend orchids amid snow flurries and pot up plants during torrential downpours. Yet get a chance to grow species you've never grown before and try new gardening techniques in a pleasant, controlled environment.

In America the first greenhouse on record was built around 1737 by Andrew Faneuil, a wealthy Boston merchant. Like his European predecessors, Faneuil used it primarily to grow fruit. The concept spread slowly, since almost all greenhouses were built for the wealthy.

Indeed, George Washington, perhaps the richest American of his day, craved pineapples and ordered a greenhouse pinery built at Mount Vernon so that he could serve fresh pineapple to his guests.

By 1825, however, greenhouses were increasingly common. Many of the greenhouses were heated by furnace-warmed air; some were pit greenhouses built into the earth and heated largely by sunlight flowing in south-facing windows. This is a design that remains highly practical today.

The modern concept of the greenhouse is simple and practical. No longer is it the private domain of the moneyed class but something that anyone can have for relatively little cost.

Today a greenhouse can go virtually anywhere there is space; it can be attached to the house, placed in the backyard, or perched on a roof or deck.

In addition, greenhouse routines are now increasingly automated, reducing the amount of time and care owners must spend. Home production of all kinds of vegetables and flowers has never been quite as easy—or as pleasurable.[9]

CHAPTER TWENTY-SIX

The Promise of Spring

See! The winter is past.
—Song of Songs 2:11

Springtime means different things to people, but in my friend Win's childhood, it meant the migration of female relatives—aunts, mothers, grandmothers—from the house into the garden.

"The women in my family were lousy housekeepers but passionate gardeners," says Win. "Since Mother was a water colorist who arranged bouquets before she dusted—a habit she passed on to me—she looked for flowers to paint, flowers to arrange, and flowers to dry and make into potpourri." As a result, Win's mother, Helen Harkness, cultivated gardens that surrounded the large, shaded patio of their ranch house in the coastal valley south of San Francisco.

As Win and each of her sisters grew to twelve years of age, they began participating in a cherished family custom. "We were handed stone jars to begin filling with fallen rose petals, lemon verbena, and lavender to make our special family potpourri, and I have never stopped," she explains.

Win says it's hard to overstate how important this potpourri-making process, handed down through the generations, was to the women in her family. Her great-grandmother, Mary Hawkins, brought the recipe from her grandparents' plantation in Alabama. Win's grandmother, Minerva Kelley, who lived on a Civil War pension and spent her later years in a two-room cabin in the prune and walnut orchard on the Harkness ranch, surrounded the small house with a fragrant garden. There she plucked and picked up flower petals, along with her daughter and grand-daughters, and saved them for potpourri.

The passing of winter stirs something within. We hear the call of the earth. It beckons with new beginnings.

"Poor as my grandmother was, she did live richly," recalls Win. "A couple of times a year she would buy a supply of beauti-ful wide ribbon, mostly white, from the local dry-goods store. She also bought narrow satin ribbon in pastels and matching embroidery thread. Remember, I'm talking about the depression years. Our narrow coastal valley was like an extended family, and when a girl announced her engagement, Grandmother got out her ribbon supplies."

Grandmother Kelley folded a piece of wide ribbon in half and embroidered a feather-stitch border along the edge, transforming the strip into a tube. Then she filled the tube with her homemade potpourri and tied it with a narrow bow of matching satin. "She made at least a dozen of these exquisite pieces for each bride. Each one had a clear design, and a box of these sachets looked truly glamorous in a time when none of us could afford glamour," remembers her granddaughter nearly sixty years later.

In the harsher climate of Wisconsin where she's raised her family, Win has found "it's harder to accumulate gallons of dried flower petals as my mother did." Fortunately, Win has a protected, south-facing garden where she's successfully grown several rose bushes and varieties of lavender, and in her small greenhouse, she nurtures lemon verbena and scented geraniums—all important to the treasured potpourri mix.

"Working hard, I can make about a gallon and a half of finished product a season," continues Win. "I always give plastic sandwich bags filled with fresh potpourri to each of my daughters and daughters-in-law, and there is just enough left for a few special gifts to friends." For Win, the size of the yield isn't as important as keeping up the family tradition.

"I can't *not* do it," she explains. "It goes deep."

I resonate with Win's sentiments. Not about making potpourri, but about the inconceivability of not gardening. When the ground thaws, the weather warms, and the last frost departs, I have to plant flowers somewhere. Whether it's in the awakening yard, an old crock on the deck, a battered window box, or a small herb pot in the kitchen, I can't *not* do it.

I suspect most gardeners feel this way. The passing of winter stirs something within. We hear the call of the earth. It beckons us with new beginnings, creative fulfillment, and delicate beauty. It always returns, bringing continuity and a place for the generations to belong. This is the faithfulness of springtime. This is a garden's promise.

A Prayer for Springtime

Lord, just as the garden is faithful to return, You are faithful through all the seasons of my life. You are a source of eternal love and my place of belonging. I thank You wholeheartedly and love You deeply for this. And I will be faithful to You. Amen.

Just as springtime is faithful to return, God is faithful and loving to us. "Know therefore that the LORD your God is God; he is the faithful God, keeping his covenant of love to a thousand generations of those who love him and keep his commands" (Deuteronomy 7:9).

Knowing His faithfulness to the generations, how can we not be faithful in return? How could we not embrace so great a love?

To create your own rose potpourri, use this family recipe
passed through the generations
and generously shared by my
friend Win. This is her shortened
version of the recipe, adapted for
today's busy schedules.

Win would be honored if
other families began a petal-
collecting tradition too.

■ GATHER ROSE PETALS as
early as possible in the morning.
Pick the flowers as their buds
open, and save every rose from
any indoor bouquet. Deep red
roses are preferable, and the recipe
can be personalized with petals
from fragrant flowers such as
honeysuckle, lavender, lemon
verbena, and violets.

■ DRY THE PETALS by
spreading them on a newspaper in
the indoor shade, turning them
every day. This prevents mildew.
When the petals are "leather dry"
but not "bone dry," place them in
a large stone jar.

■ ADD DRY PETALS to the jar
throughout the growing season,
until the combination of rose and
other petals equals one gallon.
About 1/4 lavender to 3/4 rose
petals works well.

■ DUST A LIGHT COATING of
orris root over the petals at the
season's end, or when the flower
collecting is finished.

■ COARSELY GRIND 1/4
ounce each of allspice, cloves,
mace, nutmeg, and a cinnamon
stick. Also grate 1/2 of a nutmeg.
Mix the spices together.

■ ALTERNATE LAYERS of the
flower stock and spice mixture in
a clean jar. Then add a few drops
of these essential oils: geranium,
lemon, nerolie, and rose. Over it
all, pour an ounce of fine cologne
or rose extract. Mix and enjoy.

Use potpourri as a gift for friends
and family, but don't forget to treat
yourself to its pampering aroma.

Potpourri can be placed in
ceramic or glass containers without lids, net or satin sachets, or
cellophane bags tied with ribbon.
Stir or massage (in the sachet)
occasionally to renew its scent.

NOTES

THE PROMISE OF PLEASURE

1. Dorothy Frances Gurney, quoted in ed. Frank S. Mead, *The Encyclopedia of Religious Quotations* (Old Tappan, N.J.: Revell Company, 1965), 212.
2. Elizabeth Barrett Browning, quoted in *The Encyclopedia of Religious Quotations*, 167.

IN THE BEGINNING

1. Elizabeth Murray, *Monet's Passion* (San Francisco: Pomegranate Artbooks, 1989), 79.
2. Barbara Damrosch, *The Garden Primer* (New York: Workman Publishing, 1988), 2.
3. Contact Georgia Shaffer at Mourning Glory Ministries, 280 Hillview Drive, Mt. Wolf, PA 17347. (717) 266-4773.
4. C. Austin Miles, "In the Garden," *Crusader Hymns* (Chicago: Hope Publishing Company, 1966), 196.
5. Martha Stewart, *Martha Stewart's Gardening* (New York: Clarkson Potter Publishers, 1991), 11. Used by permission of Clarkson N. Potter, a division of Crown Publishers, Inc.
6. Katharine S. White, *Onward and Upward in the Garden*, ed. E. B. White (New York: Farrar, Straus, & Giroux, 1958), viii-ix. Used by permission. Excerpts from the Introduction by E. B. White to ONWARD AND UPWARD IN THE GARDEN by Kathrine S. White. Copyright © 1979 by E. B. White as Executor of the Estate of Kathrine S. White. Introduction copyright © 1979 by E. B. White. Reprinted by permission of Farrar, Straus & Giroux, Inc.
7. Eleanor Perényi, *Green Thoughts* (New York: Random House, 1981), 80.
8. Editors of Time-Life Books, *Complete Guide to Gardening and Landscaping* (New York: Prentice-Hall, 1991), inside front cover.
9. Horace, quoted in *The Concise Oxford Dictionary of Quotations* (Oxford: Oxford University Press, 1981), 125.
10. Francis Bacon, quoted in *The Concise Oxford Dictionary of Quotations*, 13.
11. Abraham Cowley, quoted in John Bartlett, *Familiar Quotations* (Boston: Little, Brown and Company, 1980), 295.
12. Ralph Waldo Emerson, quoted in Linda Joan Smith, *The Potting Shed* (New York: Workman Publishing, 1996), 48.
13. Alfred, Lord Tennyson, "A Flower in the Crannied Wall," quoted in *A Victorian Posy* (New York: Harmony Books, 1897), 39.
14. Thomas Edward Brown, quoted in *Familiar Quotations*, 603.
15. Celia Thaxter, *An Island Garden* (Boston: Houghton Mifflin Company, 1988), 4.
16. Charles Dudley Warner, quoted in *Familiar Quotations*, 603.
17. Rudyard Kipling, quoted in *Familiar Quotations*, 710.

THE GOOD EARTH

1. Marjorie J. Dietz, ed., *10,000 Garden Questions* (Avenel, N.J.: Random House Value Publishing, 1995), 1.
2. Dietz, *10,000 Garden Questions*, 4.
3. Janet Cave, ed., *The Time-Life Complete Gardening Handbook* (Alexandria, Va.: Time-Life Books, 1995), 3.
4. Adapted from Cave, *Gardening Handbook*, 2.
5. Abel Carriere, *Entretiens familiers sur l'horticulture* (n.p., 1860), 11-2.
6. Richard Brettell and others, *A Day in the Country* (Los Angeles County Museum of Art, 1984), 209.
7. *Sudbury Soil Test Kits* (Phoenix: Sudbury Consumer Products Company, 1993), 3. Used by permission.
8. Adapted from *Sudbury Soil Test Kits*, 3-5. Used by permission.
9. History drawn from The Butchart Gardens website, located at http://www.com/butchart/history.html.
10. Adapted from Editors of Time-Life Books, *Perennials* (Alexandria, Va.: Time-Life Books, 1995), 39-40.

11. Annual and biennial lists adapted from Editors of Time-Life Books, *Easy Beauty with Annuals* (Alexandria, Va.: Time-Life Books, 1996), 102-51.

12. Francis A. Schaeffer, *Pollution and the Death of Man* (Wheaton, Ill.: Tyndale, 1970), 74.

13. Cave, *Gardening Handbook*, 6.

14. Adapted from Cave, *Gardening Handbook*, 7.

15. Editors of Time-Life Books, *Organic Vegetable Gardening* (Alexandria, Va.: Time-Life Books, 1996), 15.

16. List adapted from Damrosch, *The Garden Primer*, 30.

CREATIVE GROUNDWORK

1. Celia Thaxter, *An Island Garden*, 3-4.

2. Susan McClure, *Seeds and Propagation* (New York: Workman Publishing, 1997), 32.

3. Wayne Ambler and others, *Treasury of Gardening* (Lincolnwood, Ill.: Publications International, Ltd., 1994), 223-6.

4. George Leslie, quoted in Jane Brown, *Gardens of a Golden Afternoon* (London: Viking, 1982), 23.

5. Jane Brown, *Eminent Gardeners* (London: Viking, 1990), 141.

6. Ethne Clark, "The Jekyll Style," *House & Garden*, July 1997, 134-5.

7. Perennial list adapted from Editors of Time-Life Books, *Perennials*, 112-61.

8. Quoted in Jane Gottlieb, *Garden Tales* (New York: Viking Penguin, 1990), 97.

THE EVERYDAY GARDENER

1. Mia Amato and the Exploratorium, *The Garden Explored* (New York: Henry Holt and Company, Inc., 1997), 76-93.

2. Amato, *The Garden Explored*, 85-6.

3. Adapted from the Editors of Time-Life Books, *Shade Gardening* (Alexandria, Va.: Time-Life Books, 1995), 10-1.

4. Cynthia Van Hazinga and the Editors of *The Old Farmer's Almanac* (New York: Random House, 1996), 35-7.

5. From the Monticello Internet site: http://curry.edschool.virginia.edu/~monti/grounds/flowergarden/fgarden.html.

6. Editors of Time-Life Books, *Low-Maintenance Gardening* (Alexandria, Va.: Time-Life Books, 1995), 76-7.

7. Christina, Rossetti, "Another Spring," quoted in *A Victorian Posy*, ed. Sheila Pickles (New York: Harmony Books, 1987), 12.

8. Quoted in Abby Adams, *The Gardener's Gripe Book* (New York: Workman Publishing, 1995), 137.

9. Adapted from the Editors of Time-Life Books, *Pests & Diseases* (Alexandria, Va.: Time-Life Books, 1995), 8-22.

10. Lewis Carroll, *Through the Looking Glass* (New York: The New American Library, Inc., 1960), 138.

11. Anonymous, *The Language of Flowers* (London: Michael Joseph, Ltd., 1968), no page indicated.

12. Lois Trigg Chaplin, *A Garden's Blessing* (Minneapolis: Augsburg, 1993), no page indicated.

13. Annual lists from the Editors of Time-Life Books, *Easy Beauty with Annuals*, 46.

14. Perennial lists from Editors of Time-Life Books, *Perennials*, 14, 30.

15. Thomas Moore, *Soul Mates* (New York: HarperCollins Publishers, 1994), 105.

16. Patricia Horan and Hillary S. S. Davis, *Garden Entertaining* (New York: Grove Press, Inc.), 7.

17. Horan and Davis, *Garden Entertaining*, 10, 18. Used by permission.

18. Plant list from Peter Loewer, "In the Garden by the Light of the Moon," *Fine Gardening*, December 1997, 63.

19. Peter Loewer, "In the Garden, by the Light of the Moon," 61.

THE FAITHFUL GARDEN

1. The Editors of Smith & Hawken, *The Book of Outdoor Gardening* (New York: Workman Publishing, 1996), 208.

2. Perényi, *Green Thoughts*, 67-8.

3. The Editors of Smith & Hawken, *The Book of Outdoor Gardening*, 231. Used by permission.

4. Stewart, *Martha Stewart's Gardening*, 15-6. Used by permission.

5. Celia Barbour, "Tool Tune-ups," *Martha Stewart's Living*, November 1997, 166, 168, 172.

6. Peter Loewer, *Tough Plants for Tough Places* (Emmaus, Pa.: Rodale Press, 1992), 46-7.

7. Peter Loewer, *Tough Plants for Tough Places*, 46.

8. Quoted in Sheila Pickles, *A Victorian Posy*, 100-1.

9. The Editors of Ortho Books, *Greenhouses* (San Ramon, Calif.: Ortho Books, 1991), 5, 8-9. Used by permission.

Selected Resources

Flower Gardening Books

Ambler, Wayne, and others. *Treasury of Gardening.* Lincolnwood, Ill.: Publications International, 1994.

Blume, James D., ed. *New Garden Book.* Des Moines: Better Homes and Gardens Books, 1990.

Bond, Sandra. *The Complete Guide to Foliage Planting.* New York: Sterling Publishing, 1997.

Carter, George. *Containers.* San Francisco: Stewart Tabori & Chang, 1997.

Clevely, Andi, and Katherine Richmond. *The Complete Book of Herbs.* New York: Smithmark Publishers, 1994.

Damrosch, Barbara. *The Garden Primer.* New York: Workman Publishing, 1988.

Dietz, Marjorie. *10,000 Garden Questions.* Avenel, N. J.: Wings Books, 1995.

Editors of *Fine Gardening, Garden Tools & Equipment.* Newton, Conn.: Taunton Press, 1995.

Editors of *Fine Gardening, Healthy Soil.* Newton, Conn.: Taunton Press, 1995.

Editors of Ortho Books. *Greenhouses.* San Ramon, Calif.: Ortho Books, 1991.

Editors of Smith & Hawken. *The Book of Outdoor Gardening.* New York: Workman Publishing, 1996.

Editors of Smith & Hawken. *The Perennial Companion Book of Days.* New York: Workman Publishing, 1997.

Editors of Time-Life Books. *The Time-Life Complete Gardener Series.* Alexandria, Va.: Time-Life Books,
   Bulbs, 1995; *Combining Plants,* 1995; *Designing Beds & Borders,* 1996; *Easy Beauty with Annuals,* 1996;
   Growing Your Own Herbs, 1996; *Low Maintenance Gardening,* 1995; *Perennials,* 1995; *Pests & Diseases,* 1995;
   Practical Guide to Garden Design, 1996; *Roses,* 1996; *Shade Gardening,* 1995; *Wildflowers,* 1995.

Editors of Time-Life Books. *Complete Guide to Gardening and Landscaping.* New York: Prentice-Hall Press, 1991.

Gershuny, Grace. *Start with the Soil.* Emmaus, Pa.: Rodale Press, 1993.

Hynes, Erin. *Controlling Weeds.* Emmaus, Pa.: Rodale Press, 1995.

Jimerson, Douglas A., ed. *Step-by-Step Successful Gardening.* Des Moines: Better Homes and Gardens Books, 1987.

Kourik, Robert. *Pruning.* New York: Workman Publishing, 1997.

Loewer, Peter. *Tough Plants for Tough Places*. Emmaus, Pa.: Rodale Press, 1992.

Martin, Deborah L. *The Rodale Book of Composting*. Emmaus, Pa.: Rodale Press, 1992.

McClure, Susan. *Seeds and Propagation*. New York: Workman Publishing, 1997.

McGrath, Mike. *The Best of Organic Gardening*. Emmaus, Pa.: Rodale Press, 1996.

Rodale, Robert, ed. *The Basic Book of Organic Gardening*. New York: Ballantine Books, 1987.

Rollin, Edwin. *All About Weeds*. New York: Dover Publications, 1974.

Schenk, George. *The Complete Shade Gardener*. Boston: Houghton Mifflin Company, 1984.

Slesin, Susan, and others. *Garden Tools*. New York: Abbeville Press, 1996.

Smith, Linda Joan. *The Potting Shed*. New York: Workman Publishing, 1996.

Starcher, Allison Mia. *Good Bugs for Your Garden*. Chapel Hill, N. C.:
Algonquin Books of Chapel Hill, 1995.

Stewart, Martha. *Martha Stewart's Gardening*. New York: Potter Publishers, 1991.

Gardening Supply Catalogs

Earthmade Products, P. O. Box 609, Jasper, IN 47547-0609; (800) 843-1819.

Gardener's Eden, P. O. Box 7307, San Francisco, CA 94120-7307; (800) 822-1214.

Gardener's Supply Company, 128 Intervale Road, Burlington, VT 05401; (800) 863-1700.

Smith & Hawken, Two Arbor Lane, Florence, KY 41022-6900; (800) 776-3336.

Seed, Bulb, and Plant Catalogs

Breck's (Bulbs), U. S. Reservation Center, 6523 North Galena Road, Peoria, IL 61632,
(800) 722-9069.

Gurney's Seed & Nursery Company, 110 Capitol Street, Yankton, SD 57079; (605) 665-1930.

W. Altee Burpee & Company, 300 Park Avenue, Warminster, PA 18991-0003; (800) 888-1447.

Shepherd's Garden Seeds (European), 30 Irene Street, Torrington, CT 06790; (860) 482-3638.

Wayside Gardens, 1 Garden Lane, Hodges, SC 29695-0001; (800) 845-1124.

Index of Topics

ABOUT THE AUTHOR

JUDITH COUCHMAN owns Judith & Company, an editorial consulting and writing business, and is a speaker and author of seventeen books. She was the creator and founding editor-in-chief of *Clarity,* a magazine for Christian and spiritually seeking women, and has served in editorial and management positions in publishing and organizational communications.

Judith has received national recognition for her work in education, public relations, and publishing and holds an M. A. in journalism and a B. S. in education. She is an avid flower gardener and, when time allows, an art history student at a local university.

She lives in Colorado.

To learn more about Judith's books and speaking,
visit her web site on the Internet at http://www.judithcouchman.com

To arrange for Judith to speak to your group,
contact CLASServices, Box 66810, Albuquerque, NM 87193
(505) 899-4283; (505) 899-9282, fax